Tap

Technique and Improvisation for Today's Tap Dancer

by Anita Feldman

Princeton Book Company, Publishers

A Dance Horizons Book
Princeton Book Company, Publishers
P.O. Box 831
Heightstown, New Jersey 08520

Cover design by Frank Bridges
Cover photos of Anita Feldman and Brian Green by Daniel Breslin. Chapter heading photos of the model, Brian Green, by Daniel Breslin
Interior design by EGADS (Editorial & Graphic Art Design Services), Cranbury, New Jersey

Library of Congress Cataloging-in-Publication Data

Feldman, Anita, 1951–
    Inside tap : traditional and innovative technique and improvisation for today's tap dancer / Anita Feldman.
        p.   cm.
    "A Dance Horizons book" — T.p. verso
    Includes bibliographical references and index.
    ISBN 0-87127-199-0
    1. Tap dancing. 2. Improvisation in dance. I. Title.
GV1794.F39   1996
792.7—dc20

Contents

PREFACE   *iv*

ACKNOWLEDGMENTS   *vi*

INTRODUCTION: HOW TO USE THIS BOOK   *vii*

1   CHOOSING THE BEST INSTRUMENTS   *1*

2   IMPROVISATION AND CHOREOGRAPHY   *7*

3   RHYTHM: THE HEARTBEAT OF TAP DANCE   *37*

4   DYNAMICS   *55*

5   SYNCOPATION   *65*

6   FASTEST FEET   *75*

7   TRADITIONAL TAP: THE SHIM SHAM SHIMMY AND TIME STEPS   *105*

8   TRADITIONAL TAP: FLASH   *127*

9   NEW TAP: ORCHESTRATED TAP   *155*

10   NEW TAP: POLYRHYTHMS   *175*

11   NEW TAP: UNUSUAL AND CHANGING TIME SIGNATURES   *181*

12   TAP FUTURES   *189*

APPENDIX I   FELDMAN'S FAVORITES: MUSIC SELECTIONS WITH NOTES   *199*

APPENDIX II   PRODUCT SUGGESTIONS   *207*

NOTES   *209*

INDEX   *213*

Preface

WHEN ASKED TO WRITE A MODERN BOOK on the technique of tap dance, I had my doubts about such a project. It is so burdensome to learn steps from notation, rather than from videotape or a live teacher. I asked myself, my students, and other teachers: What can I give in a book that cannot better be given in another form?

I realized that what I can best offer are concepts, ideas, and combinations that can help the dancer with two aspects of the art form of tap dance: musicality and creativity.

Tap dance evolved from many individuals who have "gotten bitten" with the joy and interest of making rhythms with their feet. It is an American art form that meshed aspects of different cultures to originate a new kind of dance. Since its beginnings in the early 1900s, it has combined the upright crisp footwork of Irish step dancing, the polyrhythmic earthiness of African dance, the complex musicality of jazz, the body shapes and poise of ballet, the vitality of street dancing from the Charleston to Break Dance, and the originality and individuality of modern dance. It has as many styles as there are tap dancers.

What all tap dancers have in common, though, is that we create rhythms with our feet. The best tap dancers should be billed as musicians, playing rich phrases of rhythms that have dynamics, expression and variety. This is the aspect of tap that I have concentrated on in this book: How can you, as a tap dancer, become a better foot musician? How can you make crisp and varied sounds? How can you be rhythmically clear? How do you dance with sensitive dynamic changes? How can you increase your speed? How can you accomplish air tricks within the musicality of the steps? These questions are answered in this book.

Beyond technique, the book assists you in becoming a creative tapper. Unless today's dancers continue to develop tap by creating new styles and new rhythms, as the best dancers did before us, tap dance will forever be limited to occasional novelty nostalgia. With the goal of inspiring creativity and open-minded experimentation, I have included an extensive chapter on structured improvisation and choreography. It is placed in the beginning of the book to encourage you to start improvising right from the start. In addition, I have included "Play" sections at the end of every chapter that suggest ways to go further with the concepts. The last few chapters describe my rhythmical experiments with tap dance, including orchestrated tap, polyrhythms, and unusual and changing time signatures. In the final chapter, I discuss the work of some other modern tap artists and predict where I see tap dance heading in the future. Hopefully these examples of developments in contemporary tap will serve as jumping off points for your own inventiveness.

Acknowledgments

MY SPECIAL THANKS TO Michael Majewski for his unfailing support and for critiquing my manuscript so thoroughly; to Rusty Frank for her invaluable suggestions and for assistance in attaining photographs; to Olga Berest, Loren Bucek, Julie Cohen, and Rhonda Price for their insightful feedback after reading and dancing through my manuscript; to musicians Gary Schall and Barb Merjan for their suggestions; to Nancy Burstein for her advice; to my parents, Lou and Jeanette Feldman, for admiring my dancing since I was five years old; to Marda Kirn and the Colorado Dance Festival for their help in tracking down photographs; to Daniel Breslin for his artistry; to Jenny Borzon for her extraordinary childcare; to the Princeton Book Company, particularly to publisher Charles Woodford for his dedication to excellence and editor Roy Grisham for his attention to detail; and to my many students over the years—including those at the Colorado Dance Festival, Columbia University's Teachers College, Olga Berest School of Dance, Montana Dance Association, University of Montana, Oberlin College, Florida Dance Festival, and Peridance Center—for the lessons they taught me.

The demonstration and chapter-opening photographs were modeled by Brian Green and photographed by Daniel Breslin.

Introduction

How to Use This Book

THE CONCEPTS, IMPROVISATION GAMES, and numerous drills discussed in this book are for tap dancers at all levels. The more complex combinations are designed for fast beginner to advanced dancers. The book is a resource to be used over an extended period of time. Hopefully, the material in the teaching chapters will continue to challenge you after the first reading. Here is what I suggest:

Start by reading the first chapter; then begin to read and work on Chapter 2, "Improvisation and Choreography." Before going on to Chapter 4 and beyond, read Chapter 3, "Rhythm: The Heartbeat of Tap Dance," but don't feel compelled to perfect everything in the chapter. Strive to understand the rhythmical concepts and notation so that you will be able to decode the combinations.

The remaining chapters should be danced through gradually in any order, depending on your interests. Feel free to jump around from chapter to chapter. Or you might try sticking with one chapter for, say, a month—understanding, practicing, and perfecting. The chapters begin simply, becoming progressively more advanced. Don't be in a hurry; expect it to take time to catch on to my notation system and to many of the combinations.

The notation for the combinations throughout the book is in five (and occasionally six) lines that go across the page:

1   the direction or other important information
2   which foot

3   the steps
4   the counts
5   dynamics (accents, crescendo or decrescendo, when applicable)
6   musical notation (only included occasionally for practice)

Chapter 3, "Rhythm: The Heartbeat of Tap Dance," explains the counts and musical notation in detail. Chapter 4, "Dynamics," clarifies the notation for dynamics.

The Notation and Vocabulary

The symbols and vocabulary are grouped according to the line on which they are found. In my notation, I use either the abbreviation or the complete word.

The symbols *, †, ‡, § may be found on any line. They indicate that additional explanation is needed. The corresponding explanation follows each combination.

Dynamics: Fifth line

f   *forte;* loud
ff   *fortissimo;* very loud
mf   *mezzoforte;* medium loud
mp   *mezzopiano;* medium quiet
p   *piano;* quiet
pp   *pianissimo;* very quiet
>   *accent;* an emphasized sound
———   *crescendo;* increasing loudness
———   *decrescendo;* decreasing loudness

Counts: Fourth line

.   An additional sound between the counts.

( )   Whatever count is inside the ( ) is silent.

1, e, &, a, 2   Any count not in parentheses is heard.

1 & a 2 & a   Triplet division is denoted by a lightface (gray) line.

- - - -   grace notes; quick sounds that directly precede the beat (the number of dashes equals the number of sounds).

The Steps: Third line

ba

Ball-tap. The entire foot is off the floor. Put ball of the foot down on floor, similar to a step, but don't put weight on it.

ba-ch

Ball-change. The weight is on one leg. Step on the ball of the free foot in back of the standing leg. Quickly change weight back to standing leg with a step on to the ball.

ba-CH

Ball-change on to a flat foot. Weight is on one leg. Step on the ball of the free foot in back of the standing leg. Quickly change your weight back to standing leg, with a step on to the whole flat foot, accenting that sound.

br

Brush. Foot is off the floor. Strike the floor with the ball of the foot as it travels in any direction—forward, back, side, diagonal, and so on. Follow through in the direction the foot is moving by bringing it off the floor after making the sound.

Bumbishay

Flap on the first foot. Put ball of foot down with second foot; slide into a DIG with second foot so that weight is on it. Step on the ball of the first foot.

ch

Chug. Foot is on floor. Lift heel as weight is lifted slightly. Slide forward slightly on ball of foot. Then drop heel. A chug is often accented. It can be done on one foot or both feet at the same time.

cl

Click. Sound is made by lifting the two toes or the two heels off the floor, and striking them together.

cla

Clap hands.

Cramp Roll

There are many cramp rolls; but the only one covered in this book is done as follows: jump off the floor, land on the first ball of the foot, then the second ball of the foot; drop the first heel, and then the second heel, ending with the weight flat on both feet. A cramp roll can be accomplished very quickly, like a drum roll.

Crawl

A traveling movement that consists of toe-drops and heel-drops with rotation of the leg.

db-le-pb

Double pullback, making four sounds. Weight is on both feet. Jump up. On your way down, brush with first foot, brush with second foot, land on first ball of foot, land on second ball of foot.

db-le-fl-ap

Double flap, making four sounds. Lift weight off the floor and perform two flaps in a row, with no pause.

db-le-sh-fl

Double shuffle, making four sounds. Perform two shuffles in a row without any pause. Do not lift knee in between the shuffles; wait until the double shuffle is completed before the knee is lifted.

dg

Dig. Strike back edge of heel into floor without putting weight on it.

DG

Dig with your weight. Leg is lifted. Dig with free foot and place weight on it. Deep sound is made with the back edge of the heel.

Double Paddle and Roll

Six sounds. With the working foot: dig, draw, dig, draw, step, heel.

dr

Draw-back. Whole foot is on the floor without weight. Lift toe slightly and brush ball of foot back so that the foot is now off the floor.

Fake Wing

The first leg is off the floor. Step on to that foot while the second foot wings to the side; brush the second foot in and step on it.

fffl

Flat-footed flap, making four quick sounds. Throw your foot down on the floor as if you were going to flap. Relax the foot and keep it flat, so that you make a roll consisting of the following sounds: ball-tap, scuff, dig, toe-drop.

fl-ap

Flap, making two sounds. Foot is lifted off the floor and knee is bent. Throw foot down to the floor, brushing the floor with the ball of the foot. Then step on to that ball of the foot. The entire step is performed as one movement: a throw and a step. Often done in a forward direction, but can be done in any direction.

hl

Heel-drop. Weight is on the foot. Heel may already be lifted, in which case, drop the heel to make a sound. If the heel is not lifted, lift it slightly, and then drop it to make a sound. Often a heel-drop is accented.

hp

Hop. Weight is on one foot. Go up into the air; land back down on the ball of the same foot, with the heel only slightly off the floor.

HP

Hop on to a flat foot. Weight is on one foot. Go up into the air and land back down on the entire flat foot, making one accented sound.

jump

The weight is on both feet. Lift your weight off the floor with both feet at the same time. Land back on the floor with both feet at the same time.

land

Weight is brought down on a particular foot after a step that goes into the air.

lp

Leap. Weight is on one leg. Go into the air and land with your weight on the opposite ball of the foot, with heel only slightly off the floor, making a sound when you land.

LP

Leap on to a flat foot. Weight is on one leg. Go into the air slightly and land with all of your weight on the opposite whole flat foot, making a sound on the landing.

Over-the-Top

Over the Top. Weight is on one foot. Hop on that foot, while the other foot slides underneath.

Paddle and Roll

Four sounds. With the working leg: dig, draw, step, heel.

pb, pullba

Pullback. Lift your weight into the air. On the way down, perform a tiny flap. Can be performed on two legs at the same time or on one leg.

pb-ch

Pullback change. Weight is on one foot. Hop in the air. On the way down, perform a tiny brush; then land on the ball of the opposite foot.

pb-CH

Pullback change on to flat foot. Weight is on one foot. Hop into the air. On the way down, perform a tiny brush. Land on opposite flat foot, making an accent.

rf

Riff, making two sounds. Weight is on one leg. With the working leg, touch ball of the foot to floor. From that position, scuff heel out to front.

rfl

Riffle, making three sounds. Weight is on one leg. With the working leg, touch ball of foot to floor, slide it slightly forward into a dig, and then draw it back.

sh-fl

Shuffle, making two sounds. Foot is lifted off the floor and knee is bent. Throw foot down to the floor, brushing the floor with the ball of the foot, following through by letting the foot come off the floor slightly until the leg is straight. Bring the leg and foot back to original position by brushing the foot in the reverse direction, and bending the knee until leg is in original position. The entire step is performed as one movement—a throw and a recover.

Sh-fl-sh-fl-sh-fl . . .

Shuffle string. Several shuffles performed without a pause and without lifting the knee in between.

sc

Scuff. Weight is on one foot. Brush the other foot forward with the back edge of the heel.

sl

Slide. A sliding sound is made according to the additional directions given following the combination.

SL

Slap. Slap your legs with your hand or hands.

sl-ap

Slap, making two sounds. Foot is lifted off the floor and knee is bent. Throw foot down to the floor, brushing the floor with the ball of the foot. Then touch the ball of that foot on to the floor without putting weight on it. This entire step is performed as one movement: a throw and touch. It is often done in a forward direction, but can be done in any direction.

st

Step. The entire foot is off the floor. Put ball of foot down on floor with heel only slightly lifted and transfer all weight to that foot at the same time.

STA

Stamp. Entire foot is off the floor. Strike floor with entire flat foot, and lift it up immediately, not putting weight on it. This is usually an accented sound.

STO

Stomp. Foot is off the floor. Strike floor with entire flat foot, and transfer weight onto that foot. This is usually an accented sound.

td

Toe-drop. Entire foot is on the floor. Ball of foot lifts off the floor with heel still on floor, and then comes down again so that the whole foot is once again on the floor, making a tap.

Tp

Tip. Weight is on one foot. Strike the floor with the front tip of the toe tap, making an accent, and then immediately lift that leg off the floor.

TP

Tip with weight. Weight is on one foot. Strike the floor with the front tip of the toe tap, making an accent, and at the same time lift your body up to transfer your entire weight onto that tip of toe.

Triple Paddle and Roll

Eight sounds made by one foot. Dig, draw, dig, draw, dig, draw, step, heel.

wing

I use the term "wing" alone to mean the sliding out to the side with either the ball of the foot, or the outside rim of the toe tap with the foot turned in.

3-s-rf

Three-sound-riff. Leg is lifted. Touch ball of foot to floor and from that position scuff heel out to front. Then heel-drop on the standing leg. You end with weight still on the standing leg; other leg is lifted and straight.

4-s-rf

Four-sound-riff. Weight is on one leg. With other foot, touch ball of foot to floor, scuff heel out to front, put back edge of heel on floor, and then drop toe.

5-s-rf

Five-sound-riff. Perform a three-sound-riff. Then put lifted leg's back edge of heel on floor, and then drop toe, changing the weight to that leg. Can be performed like a walk.

7-s-rf

Seven-sound-riff. Perform a five-sound-riff, but rather than changing the weight to the riffing foot, keep your weight on both feet. Do two heel drops, first on the original standing leg, and then on the riffing leg. As you do your last heel-drop, change weight to that leg. Can be performed like a walk.

3-s-r-rf

Three-sound-reverse-riff. Weight is on one leg. With the other foot, dig heel, draw-back, and then do a heel-drop on the standing leg.

4-s-r-rf

Four-sound-reverse-riff. Weight is on one leg. With the other foot, dig heel, draw-back, step, and heel-drop. Same as a Paddle and Roll.

5-s-r-rf

Five-sound-reverse-riff. Perform a three-sound-reverse-riff, then step and heel-drop with the free foot, changing weight at the same time.

7-s-r-rf

Seven-sound-reverse-riff. Perform a five-sound-reverse-riff, but end with weight on both feet. Heel-drop with original standing leg, and then with riffing leg. As you do your last heel-drop, change your weight.

3-s-w

Three-sound-wing. Slide leg or legs out to side while lifting entire weight off floor. Flap foot or feet into center as weight comes down. Can be performed on one leg or two.

5-s-w

Five-sound-wing. Weight is on both feet. Slide both feet out to the side, lifting weight off the floor. On the way down, brush one foot in, the other foot in, land on the first foot, and then the second foot, ending in original position with weight on both feet.

Which Foot: Second line

B, BO

Both. Sound is made by both feet or hands at the same time.

L

Left. Sound is made with the left foot or hand.

R

Right. Sound is made with the right foot or hand.

Directions: First line

arrows

Indicates direction of movement of your foot or part of your foot when looking down at your own feet.

ba

Back or backward.

beg

Begin.

clock

Clockwise. Turn or circle in the clockwise direction.

cont

Continue. Continue in the same direction.

counter

Counterclockwise. Turn or circle counterclockwise.

cr ba

Cross back. Working leg crosses in back of standing leg.

cr fr

Cross front. Working leg crosses in front of standing leg.

diag

Diagonal. In a diagonal direction.

fr

Front.

face R or L

Face right or left.

forward

Travel forward or move in a forward direction.

pos

Position.

to R or to L

Travel to right or left while continuing to face front.

tog

Together.

trav

Travel.

. . . .

Directions continue until dots end.

/

Used as a division mark so that you know that the next instruction refers to the next step.

Most of the combinations are designed to repeat immediately. Following each combination, I will tell you whether it changes sides on the repetition or does not.

I have used an asterisk, dagger, double dagger, or "section" symbol to indicate any parts of the steps that need additional explanation. (For examples of the symbols, refer to page xii.) Look for these explanations. In Chapter

6, "Fastest Feet," don't overlook the myriad technical tips following the combinations designed to help you gain speed.

It never ceases to surprise me how differently people learn dance steps. Some of my students ask me to sing syllables, or "scat," while they dance; others can learn only if I count the rhythm. Then there are those who need to get the footwork first and worry about the rhythm later. For that reason, once you are ready to learn the combinations in this book, you should figure out the method that works best for you. First, try looking at the rhythm, clapping it or making up syllables to sing it. Then figure out the footwork, keeping the rhythm in mind. If this method doesn't work for you, start by trying the footwork; then, later on, master the rhythm.

I cannot stress enough how much solo practice and assimilation helps. Even if you practice only ten minutes a day, you will hear and feel the difference. There are two major problems with expecting to improve merely by taking classes. First, it is impossible to hear yourself in class. Can you imagine learning to play the piano without hearing yourself? Second, it is so easy to depend on others to remember the steps that you might never really know the combinations until you get onto that tap floor by yourself.

Speaking of tap floors, what do you do, as is the case with most of us, if you don't have a suitable floor to practice on? You've slipped on your tile bathroom floor and danced silently on your rug. Or, your downstairs neighbor vows he will call the police the next time you take out those tap shoes.

My recommendation, if you can dance at home, is to go to a lumber store and buy either a 4 x 8 sheet of plywood or a sheet of tempered masonite. If you don't have room to keep it down on the floor permanently, get a sheet that is a quarter-inch thick so you can easily store it. If you don't need to move your dance floor, you should purchase a sheet at least a half-inch thick, which will warp less than a thinner sheet.

Another home portable floor is called a "tap mat." These have been sold by various companies for years. They are made of slats of oak, fastened on to canvas, so that they can be rolled up when not in use.[1]

If that neighbor is still giving you problems, ask your local dance teacher if she would rent her studio to you for practice. This is really the best option because you will then have a mirror, much more space, and no phone calls, cookies, or other tempting interruptions.

One exciting aspect of tap dance is that there are endless possibilities of rhythms, steps, and styles. I have only tapped the surface in this book. Always feel free to make your own creative changes on any combinations, perhaps making them easier, more difficult, or just more "you."

Another area in which you can define your own style is in the body movement. You might choose to use your movement to support the rhythms. Paul Draper put it best when he wrote, "What the eye sees is sharpened by what the ear hears, and the ear hears more clearly that which sight enhances."[2] Or you can choreograph body shapes and any style of dance movement to layer with or against the sounds. I leave the body movement for you to design.

Learning and perfecting all of the steps in this book will take you a while. Add to that all of the possible variations you can make using my suggestions, your own ingenuity and your two feet, and this book will keep you tapping for a lifetime.

I

Choosing the
Best Instruments

Shoes

THE QUESTION I MOST OFTEN GET from audiences is, "Why do you, being a woman, wear shoes with a flat heel?" I have two reasons for doing that. First, I can't even walk in heels, let alone dance. The second more serious answer is that shoes with a broad flat heel are a better musical instrument. Perhaps one reason there have not been as many great women tap dancers is that women were always trying to compete in inferior shoes.

The goal of an expert tap dancer is to elicit a variety of timbres from shoes, ranging from the deep bass of the heels to the light click of the toes. Any dancer can make a deeper, more resonant heel sound with greater contrast to the lighter toe sound, if he and she wears a shoe with a flat heel, versus one with a small, high heel.

I recommend buying leather shoes. They last longer, and they are more flexible. The thicker the sole and heel, the louder the sound. Many dancers have more than one pair of shoes—one with a thin sole for gentle, light sounds, and one with a sole that has been built up by a shoe repair person to produce a louder, more resonant sound.

There are some wonderful shoes on the market designed specifically for tap dance.[1] You can also look around at general shoe stores or in the back of your closet for a leather, low-heeled, not-too-pointed pair. The heels should not indent at all; if they do, you won't be able to do any step that involves a heel click. The only other requirement is that the toe and heel have a standard shape (in order to match the shape of the taps).

Taps are available in a variety of sizes. Many professional dancers choose Capezio Teletone Taps, which attach by screws rather than nails, thus giving you greater flexibility of sound. You can loosen the taps slightly for a more "live" sound, or you can tighten them for a crisper sound. (You know you are really hooked on tap dancing when you carry around little screw drivers everywhere you go.) Be sure the taps match the edges of the heels and the toes. The taps should not overlap or indent from the shoe.

It is a good idea to have your shoe repair person glue a thin piece of rubber on the sole of the shoe, from the back of the toe tap to about the arch of your foot. This makes the shoe more comfortable, in addition to preventing slippage on a slick floor. Be sure the rubber is thinner than the tap, or you won't make any sound.

Despite the fact that I'm giving you all these recommendations, keep in mind that individual taste is very important when it comes to shoes (and everything else in tap dance). I have known great tap dancers who wear built-up shoes with the largest possible taps barely attached, and equally great dancers who wear the tiniest cleats nailed firmly to the soles. In some of my dances, I have used beautifully designed wooden taps to get a less metallic sound.[2] Perhaps some day I will make a dance in which each of the four taps has its own timbre.

The two incontrovertible rules are: make your shoe and tap decisions by listening to yourself; and do not be afraid to experiment.

Floors

The shoes you dance in can be compared to the mallets a drummer uses. The floor is like the drum. You can choose your shoes very carefully; but, unfortunately, you don't always have control over the floor. Every tap dancer has his or her floor stories. The most memorable one for me was when I was giving a lecture-demonstration in a factory on tempered masonite boards that were taped together. As soon as I started dancing, a corner of the tape got stuck to the bottom of one of my shoes, and the tape started to wind around my shoe. Despite my improvisatory efforts to shake it off, the tape continued to climb up my leg. Some wonderful, new flash steps not duplicated since finally got me untangled.

For those times when you have a choice, your best "drum" is one that is resilient and resonant. There are two aspects of the floor that determine these qualities—what the floor is made of and what is underneath the floor.

The best floor is one made of hard wood. Maple is the least likely to splinter. Oak is also an excellent floor for tap dance. The floor should be unvarnished and unwaxed. Because maple is so strong, it does not need any sealer.[3] Other floors require appropriate sealers to protect them from water damage and warping.[4]

In addition to providing a good sound, hardwood floors made of oak or maple, versus those of soft wood such as pine, are least likely to get damaged from the stress of tap dancing. To prevent unnecessary gouging of any floor, every time you dance, be sure no edges of screws stick out from the taps.

Even more important than what the floor is made of—but harder to determine—is what lies under the floor. It will not take you long, however, to hear it in your tap dancing and feel it in your body. When a wood floor is laid directly on concrete, the sound produced is a primarily nonresonant click, with little variation in pitch between the heel and the toe. Common injuries resulting from dancing on such a floor are hairline stress fractures, especially in the knees and ankles; lower back pain; and shin splints. The last are felt as pain in the front of the lower leg caused by leg muscles tearing from their origins.[5] Therefore, try not to dance regularly on a floor laid directly on concrete. This should be the first thing to check if you start having pains in your knees, back or legs.

What you should look for to get resilience for the body and resonance of sound is a hardwood floor with air space below it. This space resembles the air space in a drum. Rather than being supported by a solid concrete slab, the floor should be supported by floor beams spaced apart, by spring coils, or by polyethylene foam—thus allowing the floor to vibrate with the dancer. This vibration, in turn, results in a more resonant sound and healthier body.

The best way to tell whether the floor is laid directly on concrete is to dance on it. See how hard it feels to your body. Listen to the sound. Are heel sounds significantly deeper than toe sounds? Are all the sounds resonant rather than being very light clicks? If so, it is time to start dancing on those new comfortable flat shoes of yours.

2

Improvisation and Choreography

THE HISTORY OF TAP DANCE is the history of tap improvisation and creativity. Influential tap dancers did not just execute the steps of others beautifully; they expanded on ideas already developed, or they came up with entirely new ideas through improvisation and choreography. The artists I consider the greatest combined virtuosity with innovation, thrilling audiences with dancing ability and at the same time expanding tap dance as an art form.

History

A good example is Bill "Bojangles" Robinson. Robinson merged meticulous technique with a vivacious and comic performance personality. A well-known anecdote that exemplifies his technique concerns an incident during a tap challenge. Bojangles asked the musicians to play an eight-measure introduction synchronized to a metronome that only they could hear. The band stopped playing but continued to listen to the metronome while Bojangles continued dancing in silence for three and a half minutes. When the band came back in, cued by the metronome, Bojangles was in perfect time.

Robinson's vital contribution, however, was his innovative development of tap. Prior to him, King Rastus Brown was the king of buck dancing. Brown used flat-footed shuffles and steps to develop countless Time Steps and seemingly miraculous breaks. "Bojangles" Robinson took the structure of

Bill "Bojangles" Robinson.

these steps—six one-bar Time Steps and a two-bar break—and brought the steps from the flat foot to his own method of dancing up on the balls of the feet. When Robinson danced on the balls of his feet, the sounds produced were crisper and clearer than any tapper's before him. There was a similarity to clogging in his upright style and method of making sound—but with the added rhythmic characteristic of swing.[1]

It is this style that tap students around the world continue to learn when they are taught traditional Time Steps. Bill "Bojangles" Robinson's contribution to tap dance was honored on May 25, 1989, when Congress instituted a National Tap Dance Day on the 111th anniversary of his birth.

John Bubbles is credited with originating a new type of tap called "rhythm tap." Bubbles created complex, swinging rhythms with syncopated accents made by dropping heels and clicking toes. He did not use regular repetitions like Robinson, but sometimes extended his phrases beyond eight bars. He was an improviser able to create innumerable variations of any step on the spot. During a tap festival held in 1980, entitled "By Word of Foot," he half-jokingly said that he improvised rather than repeating set steps, so that no one could steal his dances.[2]

Honi Coles, stylistically a very different dancer from John Bubbles, further developed the idea of extending the phrase beyond eight bars. His phrases were lyrical and lengthy, extending through the bar to make sixteen-bar phrases. Coles often concentrated on fast, subtle footwork below a beautifully turning and traveling body. In contrast to that speed, he is well known for his soft shoe, the slowest dance ever, choreographed and performed about 1946 with Cholly Atkins, his partner at that time. Much of Coles's and Atkins's act was carefully choreographed, although they were expert improvisers as well.

I consider Steve Condos's greatest innovations to be the percussive music of his tapping. In his later years, Condos took the audience on a journey of a capella rhythms without moving from a four-foot by four-foot square.[3] Greatly influenced by his older brother, Frank Condos, who created the Condos concept of percussive dance and who firmly believed in a foundation of practice and drills, Steve developed a stimulating and systematic technique that he called "rudiments."[4] As a drummer does with his sticks, Steve produced innumerable mathematical variations on how many strikes

Steve Condos in 1988, at age 70. Contributed courtesy of Lorraine Condos.

each foot can do in a row, and in what order. For instance, he would start by practicing the following step at faster and faster speeds:

R	R	L back		L	L	R	R
ball	heel	brush	pause	ball	heel	ball	heel
1	2	3	(4)	5	6	7	8

He would then double each foot strike, creating a new combination:

				back	front		
R	R	R	R	L	L		
ball	ball	heel	heel	brush	brush	pause	pause
1	2	3	4	5	6	(7)	(8)

L	L	L	L	R	R	R	R
ball	ball	heel	heel	ball	ball	heel	heel
1	2	3	4	5	6	7	8

Steve Condos would, once again, practice the combination at lightning speed, getting as fast as a drummer does with a drum roll.

Making variations was an endless and exciting process. Each time he changed an accent or added a pause, Condos created a totally different feeling and expression of the rhythm. He would, as he called it, "sculpt" the rhythm. He would practice these numerous combinations so that he could perform them fluidly and draw on them at any point for his improvisational performances.

In addition to systematic practice, Condos developed many of his ideas by improvising in front of a video camera. Upon realizing that he had done something new, he would go back, look at the step, practice it, and make variations on it—thereby, once again, increasing his range for improvisation.[5]

The tappers mentioned above were proud to be called "Hoofers," because they focused primarily on the rhythms and syncopated music of their feet. Other tap creators melded complex foot rhythms with different styles of movement and music to originate new forms.

Fred Astaire.

Paul Draper knew from the beginning of his dance career in the 1930s that he wanted to create a new expression of tap. In the late thirties, he became interested in trying to make tap dances to the style of music he loved as a child: classical. After experimenting and deciding that traditional tap steps did not go with classical music, he took ballet classes and worked in the studio on rhythms and movements that would blend with classical music.[6] Gradually he developed a new style which came to be known as "ballet tap."

Many would say that Fred Astaire is the most famous tap dancer. In addition to being marvelous to watch, he developed a new, amalgamated style of dance, cool and debonaire, which combined the full body movement of ballet, the romanticism and grace of ballroom dance, the syncopated sound of tap dance, and the percussiveness of jazz dance, creating what he called his "outlaw style."[7] Another unique aspect of Astaire's work was that each dance had to both develop a new idea and further a particular story line. His dances ranged from off-balance, tilted steps as if performed on a rocking boat (*Royal Wedding*), to playing drums with every body part (*Easter Parade*), to a dance in tribute to "Bojangles" Robinson with overpoweringly large dancing shadows that sometimes went their own way (*Swing Time*). Astaire's dances on film were meticulously choreographed, partially by him and partially by the dance directors; but he also had experience with improvisation. In 1935, Astaire emceed a radio show in which he was expected to tap a new and interesting dance each night. This became his opportunity to gain expertise in improvisation.[8]

Eleanor Powell, at age sixteen and after five years of ballet study and acrobatic training, took her first tap lesson from the noted tap dancer, Jack Donohue. In order to counteract her ballet lift, Donohue held her legs down as she danced, causing her to tap very close to the floor.[9] Growing out of this varied dance training and her admiration for the dancing of "Bojangles" and the music of Fats Waller, she developed a spectacular style of melding intricate footwork with balletic whirling turns, dynamic movements, and acrobatics.

Powell is best known for her seven-year film career at MGM. Each movie includes magnificent dance productions with dozens of men and myriad, fantastic sets that always featured Powell's original rhythmic tap. Powell prided herself on choreographing her own dances.[10] Just as Fred Astaire did, she strived to make each dance different, while remaining within her style. For instance, in *Rosalie*, Powell performed a drum dance on an arc of drums ranging from tiny to huge, which served as both stairs and musical instruments. In *Honolulu*, she combined the percussiveness of Hawaiian music with the sexiness of hula dance with tap.

Powell's dancing career ended when, at age thirty-two, she married actor Glenn Ford and had a son. She said at the time that she felt she had no choice. A woman's role in society was probably the main reason why there were fewer women tap dancers than men in the 1930s, 40s, and 50s.

The way dancers learned to tap dance during tap's golden era (from 1900 through the 1950s) fostered this important idea of developing one's own style. As dancers advanced, they no longer took classes. Some worked with coaches who assisted them in developing their own individual style. But most, with so much tap on Broadway and in clubs, learned by watching each other and by doing what they called "stealing steps." Stealing steps wasn't the same as learning steps from a teacher today, where the goal is to do the step exactly as the teacher does it. The goal—and, at that time, the unwritten law—was to get ideas from the steps, but to use one's own originality to make the step new, truly the dancer's own. Dancers would watch each other like hawks during performances to be sure that no steps were actually being stolen.

Starting around 1920, The Hoofers Club, in New York City's Harlem, was the place for dancers to steal steps. Both well-known and novice dancers ventured through a gambling/pool hall to reach the fifteen-square-foot back room that was the unofficial headquarters of tap dance. The owner, Lonnie Hicks, happened to have the extra space and liked tap dancers, so he let the dancers practice twenty-four hours a day.

Aspiring tappers would hang around, waiting for such experts as King Rastus Brown or Bill Robinson to show up, so they could steal steps. Many great tap dancers started as novices at The Hoofer's Club, among them, Leonard Reed, John Bubbles, Baby Lawrence, and Ralph Brown. They would steal what they could, then spend hours practicing on their own, developing their virtuosity and personal style.[11]

Jimmy Slyde. Photo by Vern Walker, courtesy of the Colorado Dance Festival.

The Role of Improvisation Today

A healthy development in tap today is that there are entire dance concerts devoted to tap dancing, as opposed to tap dancing being a "novelty number." Often, when one goes to see a rhythm tap concert, several tap artists are on the program. Featured along with the dancers are a small group of jazz musicians. Each artist performs individually in his and her own style to music given the musicians to play. Improvisation is usually an important part of the performance. Dancers have short rehearsals with the musicians in the afternoon, to get used to the floor and to set tempos. One of my most memorable moments was watching Jimmy Slyde rehearse before a performance that I was a part of at the Colorado Dance Festival. He got up from his seat complaining how tired he was, how he really wasn't going to rehearse. He gave the sheet music to the musicians; the music started, and he began to move. An inspiring dance evolved which combined Slyde's signature slides, fleet footwork, and graceful traveling movement. As Marda Kirn, director of the Colorado Dance Festival, said, Slyde wasn't dancing the dance; he *was* the dance. That night, I watched Slyde's performance from backstage. He did a new dance, one completely different from the one he had done that afternoon. And his entire performance was improvised!

Most rhythm tap artists perform their own combination of choreographed sections and improvised sections. Just as they once did, the other performers wait in the wings—watching, laughing, applauding, and, if they are able, stealing.

In the movie *Tap*, Gregory Hines had to talk the director into allowing him to improvise rather than having everything choreographed. To gain more respect for his improvisation, Hines calls it "improvography," denoting the combination of improvisation and choreography.

Despite the importance of individual creativity in professional tap dance, it is seldom fostered in today's classes, where most people learn how to dance. Tap classes usually consist of the leader demonstrating and then breaking down set steps, so that students can duplicate them as closely as possible. In my travel, I have found that the idea of incorporating opportunities for beginning, or even advanced, tappers to develop their own style and learn how to improvise is resisted by both leaders and dancers.

You may have experienced that terrifying moment when your tap teacher says, "Let's improvise." Out of the blue, the leader gives the frighteningly amorphous instruction to beginning dancers to be creative and "trade eights." To trade eights, the dancers stand in a circle with each dancer improvising for a specified number of bars of music. Each dancer must keep time and come in on the right beat. There is also the pressure put on the dancer to do something "fancy."

The result of this dip into improvisation without first working on the necessary skills is that both dancer and teacher is frustrated and dissatisfied. The leader promptly gives up improvisation and returns exclusively to rote learning. He or she is left with the uncomfortable feeling that improvisation is only for the talented, creative few.

Believing firmly that it is vital to develop a student's creativity along with his or her technical ability, I start giving simple improvisation exercises within the first few classes. When I first began introducing improvisation regularly, my students would groan, "Oh, not again!" But, as their confidence and skill grew, so did their enjoyment. Now it's the first thing they ask for.

If you start improvising gradually, giving yourself very specific assignments, I think you will also find it fun and challenging—and a wonderful way to develop your tap-dancing skills. In addition, you will begin to find your own tap-dance personality.

Developing Your Own Style

Hopefully, you will now agree with me that all tap dancers should develop creative ability along with technical ability. If you do, start your improvisation training as soon as you can perform a few basic steps. Even if you only know how to do a shuffle and step heel, infinite rhythmic variations are possible on these two steps alone. If your dance class does not include improvisation by the fourth or fifth session, you're missing out on one of the most enjoyable and rewarding aspects of tap dance.

This section introduces a number of improvisation "games," described progressively from the most basic to the most advanced. From these exercises, you will learn the skills necessary for improvisation, as well as improvement of your technique. After the description of each "game," I have clarified what skills you should attain. I then describe more advanced variations that you could perform. I expect and hope that you will make your own variations too.

You'll probably want to start by taking one improvisation game at a time, working through the game until you feel comfortable. In your next session, you should return to it, but this time add a variation or two. You might skip ahead to the next game, then return to an earlier one, or perhaps try another variation. The order in which you progress, how long you spend on each game, how many variations you work through—all are up to you. Repeating exercises promotes learning; since improvisation is rich in possibilities, each repetition of a game will be new and will offer fresh solutions of rhythm and movement.

If you find that there are concepts in a particular game that you don't understand, refer to the appropriate chapter to get more information. At the end of this section, I give choreography assignments related to each improvisation. If you are having trouble improvising, skip to that section and approach the ideas through choreography.

Improvisation is the most fun when it can be done with someone else or in a group. Most of the improvisation games are for more than one dancer. See if you can get some of the other dancers in your class to join you. Even two dancers will be enough. If you are at the beginner level, try to find a leader who has more tap experience, or ask your teacher to lead the group in these activities during class. It is a lot like playing tennis: if you play with someone more advanced, you will advance more quickly. If you want to work on improvisation by yourself, most of the games can be adjusted.

Improvisation Games

"Follow the Leader"

BASIC "FOLLOW THE LEADER"

A good place to start learning to improvise is to play "Follow the Leader." Stand in a circle or a group. To music, the leader improvises one four-count phrase. In the next four counts, the others copy this improvisation as a group. This should go on continuously—four counts for the leader, then four counts for the group. Begin by using steps you all know, such as flaps, stomps, and step heels, in varying combinations and rhythms. Also, work on whatever rhythmical ideas have been stressed in your class, but this time in new variations. Start simply and build from there. It is especially enjoyable when the leader puts in rests, particularly at the beginning of the phrases.

Master tap teachers LaVaughn Robinson and Gregory Hines often end their classes with "Follow the Leader." Usually the last phrase they do in the game is something impossible for students to copy, causing everyone to laugh and be motivated for the next class.

Goals   Although this activity requires only the leader to improvise, it helps the followers begin to develop skills necessary for improvisation, such as:

1. Listening to rhythms (without added explanation or description).
2. Watching (without added explanation or description).
3. Quickness of response.
4. Accurate hearing of the tempo, beat, and measure of the music.
5. Accurate feel for the measure; learning how to come in at the proper time.
6. Facility of the feet to make rhythms.

Because you must respond so quickly, you might not get the combination exactly right. Don't be discouraged; that is actually the beginning of improvisation—making variations! Total accuracy of following is not the major goal of "Follow the Leader."

Blind "Follow the Leader"

Perform "Follow the Leader," with the followers facing away from the leader. The followers will strive to reproduce the *rhythm* of the step, with all its nuances of tone and dynamics, rather than the step itself.

Goals   This game will help you develop the ability to listen, rather than depending solely on seeing, in addition to showing you a way to start making variations.

Extended "Follow the Leader"

Play "Follow the Leader" with phrases that are two measures or eight counts long, instead of four. This game will help you develop a memory for longer phrases.

"Follow the Leader" without Music

Play "Follow the Leader" without music. This will require everyone to hold the beat steady. *You* are now the music. For an added challenge, the leader should be sure some of your phrases contain rests.

"Follow the Leader" in Unusual Measures

With or without appropriate music (see Appendix I for musical selections), play "Follow the Leader" in measures of five, six, or seven. Be sure to keep the measure of your choice constant. For instance, if you are working in measures of five, the leader improvises a step in five counts, and the followers respond immediately by copying the step in five counts with no added pauses.

Duet "Follow the Leader"

Play any of the above "Follow the Leader" games with a partner, so that everyone gets a chance to lead. Even if you don't feel ready to lead, following along will help get you used to dancing by yourself to prepare you for the more advanced improvisation games. Before you actually lead, you might need to proceed to the more advanced improvisation games that follow, so you can become comfortable with making up combinations on the spot.

Nursery Rhymes

Basic Nursery Rhymes

Choose a children's song, such as "Row, Row, Row Your Boat" or "Twinkle, Twinkle Little Star." Have everyone sing it, while each person gets a turn improvising a dance that makes a sound on every syllable of the song, so that you create the same rhythm with your feet as do the words. Try to create the feeling of the melody with your feet. As you keep repeating the exercise, strive to use unusual steps to make the sounds.

Goals   You will learn to hear and duplicate simple and familiar rhythms and melodies with your feet in creative ways. This will help you get used to the idea that your feet can be musical instruments.

Demanding Nursery Rhymes

Do the same game as above; but this time, give each other challenging demands. For instance, everyone must travel as they do their dance, or they must turn, or go up in the air, or use only the balls of their feet, or their feet can't come off the floor, and so on. The rhythm, however, must still duplicate the rhythm of the song exactly. Everyone should have several turns at each demand.

Goals This game will push you further in finding originality in the simplicity of the rhythm.

Duple Division

Using appropriate music, take turns tapping the following rhythm with steps of your choice.

1	&	2	&	3	&	4	&	1	&	2	&	3	&	4	(&)

The next person should come in immediately after two measures. When you get used to the game, challenge yourself by using less repetition in your footwork. For example, the following combination uses repetition in the footwork.

R	R	R	R	L	L	L	L	R	R	R	R	L	L	R	
dg	dr	st	hl	dg	dr	st	hl	dg	dr	st	hl	st	hl	STO	
1	&	2	&	3	&	4	&	1	&	2	&	3	&	4	(&)

The next combination does not use much repetition.

R	R	R	R	L	L	R	R	R	L	R	L	R	L	L	
dg	dr	st	hl	st	hl	sh-	fl	ball-	ch	st	dr	hl	fl-	ap	
1	&	2	&	3	&	4	&	1	&	2	&	3	&	4	(&)

The second example would be more sophisticated improvisation.

The duple improvisation game might at first glance seem very limited, but the possibilities of steps, accents, dynamics and phrasing are endless.

Goals You will gain a practical understanding of duple division of the beat and how it fits with appropriate music. It is also a simple way to help you feel comfortable with improvising and to help you develop variety in your footwork.

Triplet Division

Play the same game as above with the following rhythm:

1 & a 2 & a 3 & a 4 & a 1 & a 2 & a 3 & a 4 (&) (a)

Quad Division

Play the same game as above, with the following rhythm:

1 e & a 2 e & a 3 e & a 4 e & a 1 e & a 2 e & a 3 e & a 4 (e & a)

Tap Scored

Compose any rhythm and play the above game. Everyone will be doing variations on the same rhythm.

Mutations

All of the mutation games require you to see and hear a combination, then improvise a variation. In a variation, some aspects of the original combination stay the same, while some aspects change.

MUTATIONS IN A GROUP

As in "Follow the Leader," the leader dances a two-bar phrase. The phrase can be from a dance everyone knows, or it can be improvised. This time, the others, rather than copying, respond with a variation that is two bars long. All players dance their variation at the same time. This will result in a cacaphony of sound, but that is fine. Everyone dancing at the same time will ensure that everyone feels comfortable with making variations. Next, the leader dances a new two-bar phrase, and everyone else responds with another variation: eight counts for the leader, eight for the group, eight for the leader, and so forth, repeated over and over, with or without music.

Goals   You will further develop your listening, watching, and responding skills. Making variations is more advanced than copying, because not only do you need to perceive the phrase, you also need to use your originality on the spot to create a slightly different new phrase. You are now really improvising.

SOLO MUTATIONS

Stand in a circle. The leader dances a phrase two measures long. The next person in the circle dances a variation for two measures. The leader again dances the original phrase. The third person dances his variation. And so it goes, around the circle.

Goals   Now you will start getting used to doing a highly structured improvisation by yourself. Getting used to dancing by yourself will take time, but it is vital.

TELEPHONE MUTATIONS

Stand in a circle. One person dances an original choreographed or improvised phrase that is two bars long. For the next two bars, the second dancer improvises a variation on that phrase. Then the third person dances a variation on the *second* dancer's phrase, and so on, around the circle. Since the phrase is always changing, this game can go on forever.

Goals   Now you will start to listen and respond to each other, instead of always responding to the leader. In the beginning, this might have been difficult, because not everyone would have been clear rhythmically. But, now that you have played many preparatory games, everyone should be ready to start responding to each other.

DEMANDING MUTATIONS

Play any of the above mutation games. The original phrase should be simple, for example:

R	R	L	L	R	R	L	
st	hl	st	hl	sh-	fl	hop	
1	2	3	4	1	2	3	(4)

Before starting, someone should call out how the variation is allowed to be made. Then each dancer should get several turns to make variations according to the instruction. The following are only a few of the demands that are possible:

> Add a flash step.
> Add a turn.
> Make it travel.
> Keep the same rhythm, but change the step.

> Keep the same ingredients, but change the rhythm. (The ingredients in my example are: steps, heel-drops, shuffles, and hops.)
>
> Put pauses in it.
>
> Make more sounds in the same length of time, but use the same ingredients.
>
> Play with duple division.
>
> Play with triplet division.
>
> Play with quad division.
>
> Play with varied syncopation.
>
> Begin the phrase in the same way, but take it somewhere new.
>
> Dance the same phrase, but play with the dynamics (including accents, loudness, softness, *crescendo,* and *decrescendo*).

Goals   Narrowing the game by making specific demands will help you get deeper into the possibilities of variation. It will also help you discover the vast range of possibilities. You will thus gain expertise in whatever the demand is, whether it be dynamics, divisions of the beat, or flash steps.

ADDITIONAL MUTATION VARIATIONS

Try any of the variations listed under "Follow the Leader" for any of the mutation games. For instance, play "Blind Mutations," "Duet Mutations," "Extended Mutations," "Mutations without Music," or "Mutations in Unusual Measures."

MEMORY MUTATIONS

The leader improvises a two-bar phrase and then tries to repeat it exactly, for a total of four bars. The next dancer makes a two-bar variation on that phrase, then repeats the variation exactly. The next dancer makes a variation on the second phrase, then repeats it exactly. And so on.

Goals   Playing "Memory Mutations" will help you develop the skill of improvising and then remembering those fabulous on-the-spot steps. This is important when you start to choreograph.

Music

FOLLOW THE MUSIC

Choose some solo piano music. Listen to it first to determine the beat and measure. Go back to the beginning of the song and listen for two measures. During the next two measures, try to duplicate any part of the rhythms you just heard. Strive to dance in time with the music. Listen especially to the right hand of the pianist, which, most likely, is playing the more complicated melody. Continue with this process of listening for two measures, then dancing for two measures, through to the end of the song. Don't worry if you have trouble staying accurate with the number of measures.

CONVERSE WITH THE MUSIC

With the music you just used, play the same game as you did in "Follow the Music." This time, instead of trying to copy rhythms, try to "converse" with the rhythms by hearing them and then responding. You have many choices of how to respond. You can copy parts of the rhythm—in other words, make variations. You can make phrases that seem to agree with what you just heard. Or you can make phrases that disagree. The only rule is: *really listen and respond.* If you are doing this with someone else, talk afterward about how each of you related to the music.

TAP WITH THE MUSIC

After repeating "Follow the Music" and "Converse with the Music" numerous times, you should really know the music you have been copying and conversing with. Now turn the music on and dance through the entire piece of music in relation to the melody that you hear. You will be listening and dancing at the same time. How you relate to what you hear is up to you—you might copy, make variations, contrast (while staying on the beat), be more complex than the music in parts, be simpler in parts, use your mind or use your instincts—but be sure you really listen and respond.

Goals   You can learn much about music and rhythm by listening and responding to music. Use the vast store of possible music to extend your dance and rhythm vocabulary. Once you become adept, choose music with several instruments, then relate to one instrument at a time. Working in this way on your listening skills will help in all your dancing, whether improvised or choreographed. These games are particularly versatile because they can be done in the privacy of your own room or with your dancing friends.

Rap Tap

Prepare five sentences that you like. Find a way to say them so that they have a rhythm and dynamic changes. One at a time, rap your sentences to the group. The group will respond by improvising phrases that have the same rhythm and dynamics as your sentence. Give everyone several chances for each sentence, so that all have a chance to work on their dance phrase or make variations. An example of a sentence that can be said with a lot of feeling and rhythm is, "WHAT DO YOU MEAN, you want to become a tap dancer?"

Goals This is a fun way to start incorporating dynamics into your improvising.

Phrase Play

CONTRACTING THE PHRASE PLAY

Find one other dancer to work with, then choose music that you both like. Improvise a two-bar phrase. Your partner responds by improvising a one-bar variation on your phrase, then repeating it immediately. Continue with your improvisation of two-bar phrases; meanwhile, your partner will be repeating one-bar variations throughout the musical selection.

Here is an example of a two-bar phrase:

R	R	L	L	L	L	R	R	R	R	L	L	R	L	L	L
st	hl	dg	dr	st	hl	dg	dr	st	hl	ba	hl	hl	dr	st	hl
1	e	&	a	2	e	&	a	3	e	&	a	4	e	&	a

R	R	L	R	R	R	L	L	R	R	L	R	R	R	L	
ba	hl	hl	dr	st	hl	st	hl	ba	hl	hl	dr	st	hl	STO	
1	e	&	a	2	e	&	a	3	e	&	a	4	e	&	(a)

And here is an example of a one-bar variation of the phrase:

R	R	L	L	L	L		R	R	L	L	L	L	R	L
st	hl	dg	dr	st	hl		st	hl	dg	dr	ba	hl	hl	STO
1	e	&	a	2	e	(&)	a	3	e	&	a	4	e	&	(a)

Repeat.

Goals   You will now get experience in improvising phrases of different lengths within the same number of counts. You will also continue to work on improving your on-the-spot memory.

EXPANDING THE PHRASE PLAY

This game is the reverse of the previous one. Once again, work with a partner. Improvise a phrase one measure long and repeat it immediately. Your partner then improvises a variation on your phrase that lasts two measures. Be sure that your partner's phrases are one phrase that lasts two bars, not two or more short phrases put together. Continue with this game throughout the musical selection.

This is an example of a one-bar phrase:

R		L	L	R	R	R		L	
st		fl-	ap	sh-	fl	st		STO	
1	(&)	a	2	&	a	3	(&)	a	(4)

Repeat.

Here is an example of a two-bar variation of the preceding phrase:

R	L	L	L	R	R	R	L	L	L	R	R	R
st	sh-	fl	st	sh-	fl	st	sh-	fl	st	sh-	fl	st
1	&	a	2	&	a	3	e	&	a	4	&	a

L		R	R		L	L		R	
st		fl-	ap		fl-	ap		STO	
1	(&)	a	2	(&)	a	3	(&)	a	(4)

Goals   Now you will begin to make longer phrases even with a limited amount of material.

COMPLETING THE PHRASE PLAY: I

Again, work with a partner. Improvise a phrase that is two bars long and that gradually increases in intensity, either by getting louder or getting denser. In response, your partner should improvise a two-bar phrase which continues from where you ended and completes your phrase, while gradually decreasing in intensity. Now it is your turn to start with a new phrase. Continue for the full length of your choice of music.

Goals   Another way to interact rhythmically with someone else is to continue where he or she left off. You will also work on phrasing and dynamics in this game. A phrase has both a shape and an aesthetic meaning. In the exercise immediately above, the shape of the phrases that you will make together is:

COMPLETING THE PHRASE PLAY: II

Improvise a phrase that is two bars long. The beginning should be very intense; then it should gradually decrease in intensity. In response, your partner should improvise a two-bar phrase that continues from where you ended and completes your phrase by gradually increasing in intensity until it reaches a climax. Then it is your turn to start again.

Goals   You will get experience in making phrases with a new shape, which is:

Dynamic Phrase Play

Phrases can have four dynamic shapes. One, they can start quietly and end loudly. Two, they can start loudly and end quietly. Three, they can start quietly, build to a climax, and end quietly. Or, four, they can start loudly, quiet down, then end loudly. Choose one of these shapes for everyone to work with. Stand in a circle. Each dancer takes turns improvising a two-bar phrase with the chosen dynamic shape.

Goals   You will get much practice in improvising phrases with dynamic changes.

Guess the Phrase Play

Take turns improvising a phrase with a dynamic shape. See if the others can guess what the shape is.

Phrase Play Variations

The phrase play games described above can be varied by improvising longer phrases, working in unusual meters, and tapping without music.

Make a Break

This game renews the original practice of the Time Step and the Break in the 1920s. As is quite common today, dancers were performing to popular tunes that were thirty-two bars in length. They would dance a Time Step six times, then improvise or choreograph their own original Break, which lasted for two bars. They would repeat these eight bars four times, with either the same Time Step Break or a variation.[12] The Time Step later became standardized, and the most popular ones, along with their Breaks, were taught throughout the country, thus losing the original creative spirit.

You need to know a Time Step in order to do the next improvisation.

Make a Time Step Break

You can play the Time Step Break game alone or with others. I will describe it as if there were a few dancers, but you can easily adjust the instructions as needed.

Stand in a circle. In unison, dance three one-bar Time Steps of your own choosing. The steps can come from Chapter 7, or they can be original. A dancer then improvises an original one-bar Time Step Break alone. In unison, everyone again dances the same three one-bar Time Steps. The next dancer in the circle then improvises a one-bar Break. Continue in this manner around the circle. Do this until everyone has had at least one chance to improvise.

Make a Longer Time Step Break

Everyone dances in unison six one-bar Time Steps or three two-bar Time Steps. Next, the first improviser creates a two-bar Break. Continue around the circle as in the preceding game.

Make Any Break

Play either of the above two games; but, instead of the unison step being a Time Step, choose any one-bar or two-bar step that can be repeated. It could be a Soft Shoe, a Paddle and Roll, a syncopated blues rhythm, or a riff combination. The repeated steps can be something that you learned in class or that one of you made up. Choose appropriate music.

Goals   By choosing various steps on which to improvise Breaks, you will gain skill in improvising all kinds of Breaks.

Demand a Break

Play any of the preceding three games. Before you start, though, someone should demand a characteristic of the Breaks that all of you improvise. For instance, demand that the Break:

> be in triplets
>
> be syncopated
>
> have at least one pause at a surprising spot
>
> have at least one count of quads
>
> combine duples and triplets
>
> include a riff
>
> include a flash step
>
> be totally different from the Break improvised by the
>   preceding dancer
>
> turns
>
> travels

MAKE AN ODD BREAK

Since we no longer have to dance to thirty-two-count music, the bars can be of different lengths. Try the above games, all in measures of fives, sevens, or nines.

One of my dances, entitled "The Next Step," which I made in collaboration with composer Gary Schall, repeats a ten-count phrase twice, then has a six-count Break. This occurs over and over, until a pattern has been established. The Break also does not have to be at the end of the repetitions; instead, it can be in the middle. For instance, you could dance two Time Steps, then the Break, then a final Time Step. Anything goes. Experimentation is the seed of interesting new developments in tap dance. Use your creativity to form unusual bar patterns.

Trading Eights

I've saved until last this more popular way of practicing improvisation I mentioned at the beginning of this chapter. You can wait to play until you have tried all of the previous games, or you can play this at any point as many times as you would like.

Actually, the main difference between Trading Eights and the other exercises is that Trading Eights allows greater personal freedom in improvising. I believe, first, that you will have more choices, and, second, that you will feel less afraid of the freedom, if you have previously played the more structured games.

TWO-BAR TRADING EIGHTS

Stand in a circle. To music, the first dancer improvises for two bars. Continue around the circle, each dancer improvising for eight counts. It is up to each dancer whether he or she makes a variation, a totally new step, a response, a contrasting step, a step that relates more to the music than another dancer, or any other option. In order to learn continually, it is best to strive to, one, listen to each other and the music; two, be aware of the decisions you and others are making; and, three, to try something different each time it is your turn. After you have been trading eights for a while, stop and share your ideas and thoughts.

Goals   Here is an opportunity to gain experience with the ideas you have been working on—but ideas that are based on your own choices. For instance, you might choose to follow the leader, make variations, make phrases that last longer than a bar, include repetitions or short phrases, use dynamics, or make contrasting steps. You might relate to each other, to the music, or to your own moment of inspiration. You might also end up discovering new ways to respond to rhythms that I haven't mentioned.

Extended Trading Eights

Try any length of improvisation, from half a bar to sixteen bars. The longer you improvise, the more demanding it is, creatively.

Trading Whatever

As always, a bar can be any number of counts—three, five, seven, and so on. Try working in any length of measure with the appropriate music.

Ostinato Trading Eights

Make a simple background ostinato pattern that you can all do together repetitively.[13] For instance,

R	L	BOTH	
step	ball	clap	
1	2	3	(4)

Whenever it is not your turn to improvise, you should be dancing the ostinato pattern.

Goals   Dancing to your own rhythms, rather than to music, will help you think of your dancing as the music itself. You will also gain skill in coming out of your improvisation directly into a set pattern. This is important if you want to incorporate improvisation into your choreographed dances.

A cappella Trading Eights

Trade Eights with no music, and with no one holding the beat or measure.

Goals   "Trading Eights a cappella" requires and develops the skills of a trained jazz musician. You must be able to hold the tempo independently while continuing the musical line without help from supporting music or rhythms.

TRADING EIGHTS DANCE

Form a longer structure to make an improvised dance. For instance, do this entire structure consecutively:

(a) four bars each around the circle

(b) two bars each around the circle

(c) one bar each around the circle

(d) half of a bar each around the circle

Figure out your own structures so that they will last an entire piece of music. Once you have become skilled at improvising, you can make all kinds of structures that incorporate improvisation and that will result in extremely interesting performance.

Choreography

In this chapter, I have concentrated on improvisation rather than choreography; but they are totally interrelated. Improvisation can be used as a stepping-stone to choreography, or visa versa.

In order to develop the bridge between improvisation and choreography, try doing any of the improvisation games I have described as choreographic studies instead. You may encounter difficulty improvising. If you do, try the game first as a choreography assignment, to give you some ideas you can later use for improvisation. Or, if improvisation comes easy to you, start by playing the games as described. After much exploration, choose from your best ideas and choreograph set phrases.

Following are some possible ways you can use the improvisation games as choreography assignments:

1. *"Follow the Leader."* Choreograph phrases you can use for leading in "Follow the Leader," or any of its variations. Take turns being the leader.

2. *"Nursery Rhymes."* Choreograph a phrase that has the same rhythm as a nursery rhyme of your choice. The rhythm will be fairly simple;

so challenge yourself by devising unusual steps. If you like, give each other demanding assignments (just as you did in "Demanding Nursery Rhymes").

3. *"Duples, Triplets,* and *Quads."* Choreograph phrases that have a constant duple, triplet, or quad division of the beat. In your choreography, challenge yourself with interesting accents and dynamics.

4. *"Tap Scored."* Score a rhythm, have a composer score a rhythm, or borrow a rhythm from a score already composed.[14] For fun and comparison, have everyone choreograph a phrase that realizes the same rhythm. See how much variety you all can get from just one rhythm.

5. *"Mutations."* Start with a phrase you have choreographed or a phrase you have learned in class. Create five different variations on that phrase. If you are stuck for ideas, look at the suggestions in "Demanding Mutations."

6. *"Tap with the Music."* Choose music with up to five instruments. Choreograph in relationship to any one instrument that you hear. Whenever you wish, switch to a different instrument.

7. *"Rap Tap."* Write a story, and figure out how it can be told with set rhythm and dynamics. Choreograph tap steps that have the same rhythm, dynamics, and feeling. Try the steps at the same time as someone raps the story. Try them in silence, then try them in a round with the story. In other words, try a step from one sentence while a friend raps a different sentence. Figure out which steps and sentences work well together. Combine all three of the above ideas into a dance that includes rapping and tapping.

8. *"Phrase Play I."* Choreograph one-bar, two-bar, four-bar, six-bar, and eight-bar phrases. Be sure the longer phrases actually take the whole time to complete and that they have no shorter phrases within them. Make a dance to music that includes phrases of different lengths.

9. *"Phrase Play II."* Choreograph phrases of any length, with all possible dynamic shapes.

10. *"Complete the Phrase Play."* Choreograph a step that has no ending. Have a friend choreograph the continuation and completion of the step. Perform the step by dancing the first part and having your friend dance the final part. These phrases can have dynamic shapes of your choice.

11. *"Make a Break."* Choreograph your own Breaks for any steps you have learned or made. Make challenging demands on yourself.

12. *"The Next Step."* Now you are on your own. Use any combination of images, music, ideas, and challenges to create phrases and whole dances for yourself and others. Try your own balance of improvisation and choreography in your dances. Put any part of yourself into these explorations—your varied interests and skills, your emotions, your perceptions, your intellect and instincts. Experiment! Creativity is actually glorified play, so don't forget to have fun—I have no doubt that you will.

By including creative development in your training, you will constantly be nourished with new ideas of your own. And you will be continuing the process by which tap dance has flourished in the past, bringing it into the future in ways perhaps that you never imagined.

3

Rhythm:
The Heartbeat
of Tap Dance

Many great tap dancers have discouraged students from counting, saying that overanalyzing can destroy the rhythmic feel. But, without a framework—such as understanding exactly when a phrase begins, or how a beat is divided, or how long a measure is—it is very hard to learn, understand, and remember rhythms. And, since you, as a rhythm tap dancer, are a musician, it is invaluable for you to have a musician's knowledge. After all, 90 percent of all musicians today read music in order to enhance their musicality and give them greater range. This knowledge will do the same for you as a tap dancer. It will also help you remember combinations, make new rhythms, and listen to and choose appropriate music.

In this book, I notate the rhythms of the tap combinations with counts. I also review basic musical notation. This will help you if you need to read a musical score and will enable you to better communicate with musicians and composers. For additional practice, I have interspersed musical notation throughout the book.[1]

The Underlying Beat
Most of the music you will tap dance to has an underlying beat. Usually you will hear this beat in one or more instruments. You will need your intuition and knowledge to figure out where the beat is.

Listen, for instance, to Thelonious Monk's "Little Rootie Tootie."[2] It is a solo piano piece. You will hear Monk playing a slow steady beat with his left hand. The right hand is playing a much faster, syncopated melody. Should you use the steady beat of the left hand as your underlying beat, or should the underlying beat be twice as fast?

As I dance with the music, I start doing running flaps.[3] The double-time tempo works much better for counting my flaps; so I choose that beat. As the music proceeds, Monk's left hand starts playing the double-time beat I have chosen. Therefore, I conclude that that is the appropriate underlying beat.

Unless you have a score, eventually you will have to determine what works best as an underlying beat. Once you have made that decision, stay consistent—unless, of course, the music does not stay consistent. For instance, the music itself might change into double-time or half-time, or the tempo might change totally.

Once you hear the beat clearly, you need to decide what kind of musical note you will use to represent one beat. For our purposes, we will always use a quarter note to last one beat. A quarter note looks like this: ♩

The Measure

Music would be very monotonous and inexpressive if there were no stressed and unstressed beats. Measures are created by periodically stressed beats, or accents, in the underlying beat. For instance, if the first beat of every three beats is accented, the measure created is a three. The majority of jazz music and popular music is organized into measures of four, meaning that the first beat of every four is accented. Music and tap dance, however, can be organized in any length of measure or in changing lengths of measures, resulting in fascinating phrasing and new expressions of tap.[4]

Even for more advanced dancers, it is sometimes difficult to know what to listen for to determine where the first beat of each measure is in the music. The first beat of every measure might be slightly louder; or perhaps the first beat will always be a particular pitch. Hearing where new melodies begin is another clue. Sometimes there is a repetitive pattern in one of the instruments, or, in the case of the piano, in one hand. Listening to the duration of that repetitive pattern will give you a good idea of how long the measure is.

The Time Signature

If you know where the beat is and how long the measures are, you have all the information you need to determine the time signature of any piece of music. A time signature looks like this: $\frac{3}{4}$

You will always find the time signature at the beginning of a musical score. The top number tells you the length of each measure, and the bottom tells you what kind of a note gets one beat. So, for this $\frac{3}{4}$ time signature, the measure is three beats long (or the first of every three beats is stressed), and a quarter note gets one beat. If the time signature is $\frac{5}{4}$, the music is organized into measures of five; and, once again, the quarter note delineates one beat. In music that has changing lengths of measures, whenever the length of the measure changes, there is a new time signature, which lasts until you see the next time signature. Rhythms with changing lengths of measures look like this:

Dancers often count steps that are in a $\frac{4}{4}$ time signature in eights instead of fours. If you start working with a composer or a musician, you will find that this can cause a problem. For that reason, I will count all combinations that are in a $\frac{4}{4}$ time signature in fours. If it is easier for you to learn them by counting eights instead, feel free to do that.

Subdivisions of the Beat

To go further with your understanding of rhythm, you now need to be able to hear the underlying subdivision of each beat. I hope to offer some helpful suggestions. There are many different methods of counting the divisions of a beat, using syllables or numbers. Below, I describe the method used throughout this book.

Each of the following notations consists of two lines. The top line is the count, and the bottom line is the musical notation.

If the beat is divided into two equal parts, it is called a "duple division." Each duple, twice as fast as the underlying beat, is called an eighth note. An eighth note looks like this: ♪

Following are the notation and counts for a measure of eighth notes. Notice how the eighth notes for each beat are attached.

Beats that are divided into three equal parts are called "triplets." Each of these notes, three times faster than the underlying beat, is a triplet eighth note. The notation and counts for a measure of triplet eighth notes are:

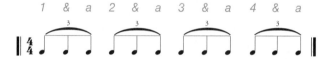

Triplets have a very different feel from duples. To be sure you can tell when a combination is in triplets, I highlight the counts for any triplets, as you can see in the example given above.

Beats that are divided into four equal parts have a quadruple (or quad) division. Each note, four times faster than the underlying beat, is a sixteenth note. The notation and counts for a measure of sixteenth notes is:

The three options above are the most common divisions; but a beat can be subdivided into any number. If a beat is divided into five equal parts, I count it with numbers only: **1** 2 3 4 5 **2** 2 3 4 5, etc. If a beat is divided into six equal parts, I count it: **1** 2 3 4 5 6 **2** 2 3 4 5 6, etc. This is the smallest division I deal with in this book.

Rests

A division of the beat does not have to be heard for that beat to have an underlying, even division. Unheard beats are called "rests."

The musical notation for some of the most commonly used rests are:

quarter note rest: ⌡

eighth note rest: ⌐̸

triplet eighth note rests: ♪⌐̸⌐̸

sixteenth note rest: ⌐̸

The most likely place at which you will get out of time with the music is during a rest. The tendency with even experienced dancers and musicians is to make the rest shorter than it is supposed to be. A good way to keep this from happening is to count in your mind the rests as well as the heard beats—therefore, count all even, underlying beats to yourself. In my notation of combinations, I include all of the subdivisions of the beat; the rests are in parentheses, meaning that they are silent.

I now give some examples of rhythms—their musical notation and counts. Each rhythm is four counts long. Practice clapping, tapping, and counting each rhythm, repeating it over and over. You should make a sound on every count that is *not* in parentheses; you should not make a sound on any count that *is*.

Duple Division

Shown by eighth notes and eighth-note rests:

Triplet Division

Shown by eighth-note triplets and eighth-note triplet rests:

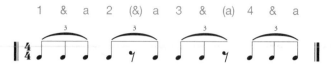

Quadruple Division

Shown by sixteenth notes and sixteenth-note rests:

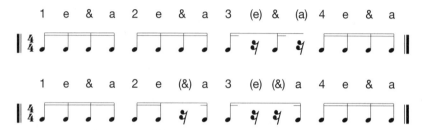

Quintuplet Division

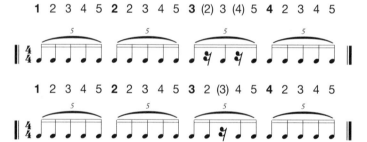

Sextuplet Division

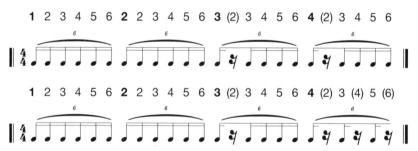

I can't stress enough how important it is that each rhythm be evenly counted. Check to be sure that you are adding no pauses before the downbeats.[5]

Phrasing

Another important aspect of music is the overall organization, or phrasing, of the piece. Ideas in music usually last a certain number of measures. This can be compared to writing, in which a paragraph expresses a single idea and consists of a certain number of sentences.

In jazz music, a measure of four beats is called a "bar." This makes sense, since, in musical notation, a vertical line or bar delineates the end of each measure. In most popular and jazz music, a musical idea lasts sixteen bars, which in jazz music is called a chorus. To complement, rather than contrast with, the music, the phrasing of your steps also needs to last sixteen bars.

However, there are many examples, even in jazz music, where the phrasing is different than you might expect. In the blues, the phrases usually last twelve bars; this is known as the "Twelve Bar Style." Occasionally, you will find that the phrasing does not stay consistent throughout the piece.

For practice, in all the music you listen to, figure out how long the phrases last. When you choreograph to music, it will be your choice when to contrast the phrasing of the music and when to go along with the phrasing. Remember, though, it is not a good idea to ignore the organization of the music.

The Rhythm of the Music

The time signature and underlying subdivision of the beat help define the kind of music you are listening to. In most jazz music—including blues, bebop, and swing—the time signature is $\frac{4}{4}$ and the beats are played mainly with a triplet feel. Jazz musicians call this feel "swinging eighth notes." Occasional duple and quad divisions are used for accents and rhythmic interest.

Waltzes of any style—jazz, classical, popular, or avant garde—are organized in measures of three. The divisions of the beat can be duples, quads, or triplets.

Jazz music that divides the beat into eighth notes and sixteenth notes is called "Straight Eighth Note Style," or simply, "Military." This is not as common as jazz music with a triplet feel. Marches and much rock music also use duple and quad divisions. All of these have a $\frac{4}{4}$ time signature.

The music you hear might not fit into any of the above categories. It can be organized in any length of measure—such as 5s, 7s, or 17s—and each beat can be divided into any number of subdivisions, limited only by the imagination of the composer and the skill of the musician.

I have found that students often have no idea how to choose appropriate music to practice the steps taught in class. They can tell that a particular piece of music isn't "right," but they don't know why. Does that sound like you? If so, your only recourse is to search for the same music the teacher is using. It would be preferable if you could learn to dance to the music that you most love. I hope that the above information will help you choose your own wonderful and rhythmically appropriate music. With this goal in mind, I list in Appendix I my favorite musical choices and analyze them according to measure length, subdivision of the beat, and phrasing. After practicing with these selections, you should be able to analyze your own musical choices.

The Rhythm of Your Feet

A tap dancer should be able to switch from duple to triplet to quadruple division at will, without changing the tempo. Innumerable exercises can be made up for this purpose.

Following are a few simple exercises as examples. Do these exercises to the beat of a metronome or drum machine, at various tempos. Sometimes slow tempos take even more skill than fast tempos; so don't leave them out. From these examples, devise exercises of your own.

BASIC RHYTHM EXERCISES

R	L	L	R	R	L	L	R
hl	st	hl	st	hl	st	hl	st
1	&	2	&	3	&	4	&
>		>		>		>	
>							

R	L	L	L	R	R	R	L	L	L	R	R
hl	br	st	hl	br	st	hl	br	st	hl	br	st
1	&	a	2	&	a	3	&	a	4	&	a
>			>			>			>		
>											

R	L	L	L	L	R	R	R	L	L	L	L	R	R	R
hl	dg	dr	st	hl	dg	dr	st	hl	dg	dr	st	hl	dg	dr	st
1	e	&	a	2	e	&	a	3	e	&	a	4	e	&	a
>				>				>				>			
>															

Does not alternate sides.

Repeat this three-measure exercise many times in a row without any pause. When you can tap it at a variety of tempos, add the following two measures to the end of the exercise; then repeat the entire exercise many times without pause.

R	L	L	R	L	L	R	R	L	R	R	L	L	R	L	L	R	R	L	R
hl	dg	dr	hl	st	hl	dg	dr	hl	st	hl	dg	dr	hl	st	hl	dg	dr	hl	st
1	2	3	4	5	**2**	2	3	4	5	**3**	2	3	4	5	**4**	2	3	4	5
>					>					>					>				
>																			

R	L	L	R	L	L	L	R	R	L	R	R	R	L	L	R	L	L	L	R	R	L	R	R
hl	dg	dr	hl	fl-	ap	hl	dg	dr	hl	fl-	ap	hl	dg	dr	hl	fl-	ap	hl	dg	dr	hl	fl-	ap
1	2	3	4	5	6	**2**	2	3	4	5	6	**3**	2	3	4	5	6	**4**	2	3	4	5	6
>						>						>						>					
>																							

The accents fall naturally on every beat, with the loudest accent at the beginning of each measure. As you do the divisions of 5 and 6, be sure that you have the major accent consistently only on the beats.[6] From this exercise, you can design others that use different footwork and that have different combinations of the divisions of 2, 3, 4, 5, and 6.

Here is an example of another rhythm that lasts two measures, with counts and notation:

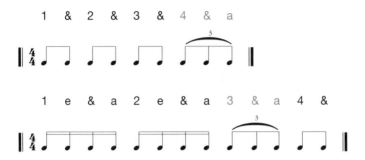

A more complicated rhythm is:

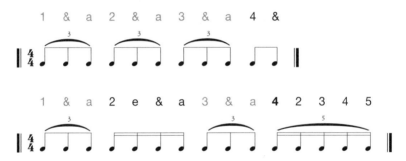

Try choreographing your own footwork to play the two preceding rhythms. When you have perfected the repetition of these patterns at different tempos, notate your own new rhythms, using varied divisions of the beat. Then devise your own footwork exercises from these rhythms.

As you tap these rhythms, you might think the tempos are varying within each exercise because you are tapping faster and slower; but they really are not. The underlying beat should be perfectly constant. It is the division within the beats that vary, making your tapping become faster and slower.

Advanced Rhythm Exercises

In the exercises just described, the heel occurs on each downbeat, making it easy to feel the accented beat. When you were doing a duple division, the step lasts two sounds. For a triplet division, the step lasts three sounds. And for a quad division, the step lasts four sounds—always with the heel on the beat.

A much more advanced way to practice rhythms with varied divisions is to make the step consist of a different number of sounds than the number of subdivisions. What happens then is that every time you hit the downbeat, you are at a different part of the step, which leads to some very interesting phrasing. You'll understand this best by trying some examples:

R	L	L	L	L	R	R	R
hl	dg	dr	st	hl	dg	dr	st
1	&	2	&	3	&	4	&
>				>			

R	L	L	L	L	R	R	R	R	L	L	L
hl	dg	dr	st	hl	dg	dr	st	hl	dg	dr	st
1	&	a	2	&	a	3	&	a	4	&	a
>			>			>					

L	R	R	R	R	L	L	L	L	R	R	R	R	L	L	L
hl	dg	dr	st	hl	dg	dr	st	hl	dg	dr	st	hl	dg	dr	st
1	e	&	a	2	e	&	a	3	e	&	a	4	e	&	a
>				>				>				>			

Notice that you are doing only one repetitive step during this entire exercise. This step is called "Paddle and Roll." What makes the exercise interesting is the accent pattern of the second measure. When you do the triplets in the second measure, be aware that the accent is on a different count of each triplet, that, at the beginning of each beat, you are at a different part of the Paddle and Roll. During the triplets, don't think of each Paddle and Roll separately; rather, think of three of them forming one four-count phrase.

Here is another example:

R	L	L	L	R	R	R	L
hl	br	st	hl	br	st	hl	br
1	&	2	&	3	&	4	&
>			>			>	

L	L	R	R	R	L	L	R	R	R	L	L
st	hl	sh-	fl	st	st	hl	sh-	fl	st	st	hl
1	&	a	2	&	a	3	&	a	4	&	a
>					>					>	

R	R	L	R	R	R	R	R	R	L	L	R	L	L	L	L
dg	dr	hl	db-	le-	sh-	fl	st	hl	dg	dr	hl	sh-	fl	st	hl
1	e	&	a	2	e	&	a	3	e	&	a	4	e	&	a
		>						>			>				

Does not alternate sides.

Again, each measure has shifting accents. Think of each measure as a phrase that lasts four counts.

Compare the preceding two combinations. Notice that they have the exact same rhythm; but the combination above is more interesting because of the accents. Dynamics and accents are important to the expression of all rhythms.

Any traditional or nontraditional step you learn can be put into a rhythmical framework that divides the beat into any number of sounds. The possibilities are endless. For instance:

SHUFFLE OFF TO BUFFALO:

(st sh-fl st)

R	L	L	L	R	L	L	L
st	sh-	fl	st	st	sh-	fl	st
1	&	2	&	3	&	4	&
>				>			

R	L	L	L	R	L	L	L
st	sh-	fl	st	st	sh-	fl	st
1	&	2	&	3	&	4	&
>				>			

R	L	L	L	R	L	L	L	R	L	L	L
st	sh-	fl	st	st	sh-	fl	st	st	sh-	fl	st
1	&	a	2	&	a	3	&	a	4	&	a
>			>			>					

R	L	L	R	L	L	L	R	R	L	R	R	R	L	R
st	sh-	fl	hp	sh-	fl	st	sh-	fl	hp	sh-	fl	st	st	st
1	e	&	a	2	e	&	a	3	e	&	a	4	&	a
>		>		>				>				>	>	>

Alternates sides.

The "Maxi Ford"
(STO sh-fl pb-ch Tip)

R		L	L	R	L	R	
STO		sh-	fl	pb-	ch	Tip	
1	(&)	a	2	&	a	3	(4)

R		L	L	R	L	R	
STO		sh-	fl	pb-	ch	Tip	
1	(&)	a	2	&	a	3	(4)

R	L	L	R	L	R	L	R	R	R
STO	sh-	fl	pb-	ch	Tip	hl	br	st	hl
1	&	a	2	&	a	3	&	a	4

L	R	R	L	R	L	R	L	L	L	R	L	L	R	L	
STO	sh-	fl	pb-	ch	Tp	hl	fl-	ap	hl	STO	sh-	fl	pb-	ch	
1	e	&	a	2	e	&	a	3	e	&	a	4	e	&	(a)

Does not alternate sides.

The first two measures are the traditional Maxi Ford rhythm. The next two measures change the rhythm in a more advanced way, requiring excellent control over your pullbacks. To learn how to gain this control, refer to Chapter 8.

Once you have perfected these exercises—as well as others you devise—you will be able to combine different divisions of the beats without thinking twice, as do today's best jazz and classical musicians. This skill will become second nature and will expand your ability to create interesting rhythms that you will know how to record and remember.

Analyzing the Steps

There is an additional rhythmical idea that I want to clarify. I have already mentioned that, when a beat has an underlying division, some of those divisions can be rests. For instance:

BUGGY RIDE TIME STEP

(Refer to Chapter 7 for more information.)

And	thanks			for		the	bug		gy	ride
dr	hop			st		fl-	ap		st	STO
a	1	(&)	(a)	2	(&)	a	3	(&)	a	4

By singing "And thanks for the buggy ride," you can easily feel the rhythm of this most common Time Step.

Many students come to me from their various classes demonstrating wonderful steps such as this one, but without any idea how the beats are divided or how to count the step. They don't really understand the step well enough to teach it to someone else, and they aren't able to choose music for it. If this sounds like you, it's time to learn to analyze the steps you love.

The key to attaining this skill is to understand clearly that even when it does not sound like a beat is being divided evenly, there is an even, *underlying* division. The important word is "underlying." You don't need to hear the evenness in the rhythm. Some of those divided beats might be silent, as they are in the above Time Step. But in order to count the step correctly you do need to know how the beat is being divided.

The first thing to do is to determine where the beat is and how long the measures are. Then experiment, singing different even divisions of the beat as you dance the step. Try putting a duple division under the step. If that doesn't fit, try a triplet and then a quad. Once again, remember that some of those even divisions will most likely be silent, and some will have sound. But only one kind of division will fit under each beat. In our Time Step, for example, each beat is divided into a triplet. Use your intuition and knowledge, and you will be able to figure out the appropriate underlying divisions of the beat and the counts of the rhythm.

Rhythm Play

1. Analyze your favorite steps in terms of their rhythm. Figure out how the beat is divided. Write down the counts the way I have for the Buggy Ride Time Step. Then find some appropriate music that is divided in the same way.

2. Once again, analyze a favorite step of yours. Try changing one count of the step by dividing it into smaller parts. For instance, if during the whole step, the beat is divided into triplets, choose one count to divide into quads. Practice this new step and feel how its expression changes.

3. Take any steps you know, such as Soft Shoe, Cincinatti, Paddle and Roll, Buffalo, and put them into rhythmic frameworks that divide the beat in a different way than you have previously learned, expanding the possible use for these steps and increasing your versatility, speed, and clarity.

4. Listen to solo piano music by Scott Joplin (this is ragtime and is sometimes a little simpler rhythmically), or by jazz musicians Thelonious Monk, Meade Lux Lewis, Jelly Roll Morton, Fats Waller, or others. Distinguish between the left hand, which is most likely holding the rhythm in a simple form, from the complex, right-handed

melody. Pick two measures of the right-handed melody, and figure out how to duplicate the rhythms with your feet. Once you have accomplished that and have memorized the phrase, analyze it and write down the counts.

5. Compose a rhythm on paper, either with musical notation or counts. Then choreograph an interesting step to play that rhythm with your feet.

6. Go to the library or music store and look at some musical scores. Notice the time signature, and see if you can read any of the rhythms.

7. Buy a score for a piece of music that you like. For practice, make new tap combinations by duplicating the rhythms that you read in the score for your feet.[7]

8. A good resource for rhythmic drills that can be transformed in many ways for the feet is the book *Stick Control for the Snare Drummer* by George Lawrence Stone (Boston, Mass.: George B. Stone & Son, 1935).

9. Find the score for the *Tap Dance Concerto* by Morton Gould (New York, 1953). It includes notated sections for a tap dancer to "play."[8]

4

Dynamics

THE QUALITIES OF YOUR TAP SOUNDS in a particular dance—whether they are gentle, violent, slurring, or crisp—add expression to your music-making on a large scale. In addition, the subtleties of accents and dynamic shadings of every rhythmic phrase make each phrase speak and bring tap dance up to the level of the finest music. These characteristics of sound are called *dynamics*.

Large-Scale Dynamics

There are two aspects to large-scale dynamics—one is the volume; the other is the quality, or timbre, of the sound.

If you listen to a variety of solo piano music, you will hear a range of volumes coming from the same instrument. Pianists can play very softly, or they can play thunderingly loud. Some of the Italian musical terms and abbreviations for different volumes are as follows:

> *pianissimo (pp)*, or very quiet
> *piano (p)*, or quiet
> *mezzopiano (mp)*, or medium quiet
> *mezzoforte (mf)*, or medium loud
> *forte (f)*, or loud
> *fortissimo (ff)*, or very loud[1]

Pianists can also change the timbre of their sound by using the pedal to slur the different pitches together—creating lyrical, romantic melodies if played quietly or whirling stormy layers of music if played loudly. Pianists can accentuate the piano's percussive qualities by playing short crisp accents and by performing music that ranges from light and lively to heavy and powerful.

As a tap dancer, you can also evoke a range of dynamics both through the sound you make with your feet and the supporting movement of your body. The first step to gaining control over your dynamics is to be able to play rhythmic phrases at all possible degrees of loudness. Try this with any phrases in the book, or with your own. When you play *pianissimo* concentrate on remaining relaxed throughout your entire body. You make quiet sounds—not tensing the leg muscles, but lifting your center of gravity. When you play *forte* it is even more important to use your whole body, rather than just your leg. Try it! Do a loud stamp, using only your leg. Then loudly stamp, supporting it with the natural movement of your pelvis into and out of the floor. I think you will feel (and even hear) the difference. Using only your legs without adjusting your weight into the floor can result in injuries and a forced-sounding loudness.

Be sure that as you start dancing at different volumes, your tempo is not affected. The natural tendencies in the beginning are to slow down when you tap quietly and accelerate when you tap loudly.

Once you have gained control over the volume of your sound, the next step is to pay attention to the quality, or timbre, of the sound. Here is where your body movement enters the picture. You may not have a pedal to blend the sounds together, but you can stretch out the gentle tapping sounds you make with arm and body movements that reinforce the continuity of the taps. If you want your steps to be loud and percussive, as they were in the stamp you just tried, reinforce the quality with strong movements that freeze between sounds.

Using images will help you create varying qualities of sound and movement. When choreographing and practicing a dance that you envision as quiet and flowing, try imagining a gently running stream or, perhaps, a calm snowfall. If you want your dance to be out of control and clumsy, pretend that you are drunk. Or by envisioning a hurricane you might create wild, loud, whirling sound and movement.

In all your dances, allow the dance to tell you what the most appropriate volume and quality of sound and movement should be. Experiment with different dynamics. A dance is not complete until the overall dynamics of the work have been fully explored and developed.

Dynamic Shadings

In addition to the overall dynamics of dance, each phrase has its natural high and low points. These subtle nuances within a combination, called "dynamic shadings," create rhythmic clarity and phrasing and can help you move the audience from one phrase to the next.

Accents

An accent is an emphasis or stress on one note.[2] The musical notation for an accent is > , which is placed under the note or, in the case of my notation system, placed under the count.

In Chapter 5, on syncopation, I demonstrate that any part of the foot can play accents. Not every accent is equal; you have a range of possible accented sounds to work with.

Following is an advanced exercise using a Paddle and Roll, to help you learn to accent any part of the step. Every two measures, the accent shifts by one sound. (For a simpler combination that shifts the accents twice, refer to Chapter 6, page 85.)

R	L	L	L	L	R	R	R	R	L	L	L	L	R	R	R
hl	dg	dr	st	hl	dg	dr	st	hl	dg	dr	st	hl	dg	dr	st
1	e	&	a	2	e	&	a	3	e	&	a	4	e	&	a
>				>				>				>			

R	L	L	L	L	R	R	R	R	L	L	L	L	R	L	L
hl	dg	dr	st	hl	dg	dr	st	hl	dg	dr	st	hl	hl	st	hl
1	e	&	a	2	e	&	a	3	e	&	a	4	e	&	a
>				>				>				>			>	

```
R   R   R   R   L   L   L   L   R   R   R   R   L   L   L   L
dg  dr  st  hl  dg  dr  st  hl  dg  dr  st  hl  dg  dr  st  hl
1   e   &   a   2   e   &   a   3   e   &   a   4   e   &   a
>               >               >               >
```

```
R   R   R   R   L   L   L   L   R   R   R   R   L   R   R   L
dg  dr  st  hl  dg  dr  st  hl  dg  dr  st  hl  hl  st  hl  dg
1   e   &   a   2   e   &   a   3   e   &   a   4   e   &   a
>               >               >       >           >
```

```
L   L   L   R   R   R   R   L   L   L   L   R   R   R   R   L
dr  st  hl  dg  dr  st  hl  dg  dr  st  hl  dg  dr  st  hl  dg
1   e   &   a   2   e   &   a   3   e   &   a   4   e   &   a
>               >               >               >
```

```
L   L   L   R   R   R   R   L   L   L   L   R   R   R   R   L
dr  st  hl  dg  dr  st  hl  dg  dr  st  hl  dg  dr  st  hl  hl
1   e   &   a   2   e   &   a   3   e   &   a   4   e   &   a
>               >               >                   >
```

```
R   R   L   L   L   L   R   R   R   R   L   L   L   L   R   R
st  hl  dg  dr  st  hl  dg  dr  st  hl  dg  dr  st  hl  dg  dr
1   e   &   a   2   e   &   a   3   e   &   a   4   e   &   a
>               >               >               >
```

```
R   R   L   L   L   L   R   R   R   R   L   L   L   L   R   L
st  hl  dg  dr  st  hl  dg  dr  st  hl  dg  dr  st  hl  hl  st
1   e   &   a   2   e   &   a   3   e   &   a   4   e   &   a
>               >               >               >           >
```

Alternates sides.

This step might seem a bit dry when you first learn it. As you get clearer with the changing accents that you will find in every other measure, you will see how accents create excitement.

Crescendo and Decrescendo

"Crescendo" means to gradually increase the volume; *"descrescendo"* means to decrease it. The musical notation for *crescendo* is:

The musical notation for *decrescendo* is:

In musical scores, all of the symbols for volume are placed under the notes. In our case, they will be placed under the counts.

Try the previous combination, starting out as quietly as you can and gradually get louder and louder throughout the eight measures. When you reach the end, suddenly get quiet as you repeat the phrase and the dynamics. You will see what life, expression, and movement this adds to a rhythmic phrase.

Now, with this same combination, try various other choices of *crescendo* and *decrescendo*. For instance, start quietly and build for the first two measures, *pianissimo* to *fortissimo*. Repeat these dynamics for the next two measures and for the two measures following. Therefore, you will have three *crescendoes* in a row. For the last two measures, reverse from *fortissimo* to *pianissimo*. Sense the difference in expression of these dynamics from the previous ones.

The choice of dynamics is endless. It is your own to make. However, it takes practice to learn to *crescendo* and *decrescendo* gradually and quickly, as well as to change volume suddenly. As I mentioned in discussing large-scale dynamics, dynamic expression demands excellent control of your weight and relaxation of the legs.

Here is a different type of combination, one that has gradual and sudden changes in volume.

R		R	L	L	R	L	L	L	L	L	L
st		hl	dg	dr	hl	db-	le-	sh-	fl	st	hl
1	(&)	a	2	&	a	3	&	a	4	&	a
pp										mp	

R	R	L	R	R		R	L	L	R	L	L
dg	dr	hl	sh-	fl		lp	5	-	s	-	riff *
1	&	a	2	&	(a)	**3**	2	3	4	5	**4**
mp											mf

*   **Refer to Chapter 6, "Fastest Feet," for instructions on how to do a 5-s-riff. Travel diagonally front and left as you do the riff. The counts are a little confusing here. Remember from the chapter on rhythm that "*3* 2 3 4 5" means count 3 is divided into five even sounds.**

Repeat three times, doing a very long extended *crescendo* over the three repetitions, from very quiet to very loud. Then do the following Break as loudly as possible.[3]

traveling to the right..

	R		R			L	L		L	R		R
	STA		STO			br	st		hl	STA		STO
	1	(&)	a	(2)	(&)	a	3	(&)	a	4	(&)	a
ff	>		>							>		>
			>									>

cont trav to R

	L	L		L	R	L	R	L	R	L	R		R
	br	st		hl	db-	le-	pb*	hl	hl	STA			STO
(1)	(&)	a	2	(&)	a	**3**	2	3	4	5	6	**4**	(&)	a
ff											>		>
													>

*   **For instructions on double pullbacks, refer to Chapter 8.**

Repeat the entire eight-measure combination on the other side. This requires you to suddenly go from very loud at the end of the combination to very soft at the beginning.

Continue with the following step.

trav R .... cross back ....trav R.......

R		R		L	L		R		R
st		hl		st	hl		st		hl
1	(&)	a	(2)	(&)	a	3	4	(&)	a

pp ———————————————— mf

.... cross fr   fr   cr   ba   & turn counter *

	L	L		R	R	R	R	L	R	L
	st	hl		br	br	ba	hl	hl	td	td
(1)	(&)	a	2	(&)	a	3	&	a	4	&	a

mf ————————————————— ff

trav R......................... cross back ....trav R.......

R		R		L	L		R		R
st		hl		st	hl		st		hl
1	(&)	a	(2)	(&)	a	3	4	(&)	a

pp ———————————————— mf

.... cr. fr.

	L	L	R	R	R	R	L	L	R	R
	st	hl	dg	dr	st	hl	st	hl	dg	dr
(1)	(&)	a	2	&	a	3	&	a	4	&	a

mf ————————————— ff

trav R .... cross back ....trav R.......

R		R		L	L		R		R
st		hl		st	hl		st		hl
1	(&)	a	(2)	(&)	a	3	4	(&)	a

pp ———————————————— mf

.... cross fr			fr	cr	ba	& turn counter *			
	L	L	R	R	R	R	L	R	L
	st	hl	br	br	ba	hl	hl	td	td
(1)	(&)	a	2	(&)	a	3	&	a	4	&	a
mf										ff

R	R	L	L	L	L	R	R	L	L	L	L
st	hl	dg	dr	st	hl	st	hl	dg	dr	st	hl
1	&	a	2	&	a	3	&	a	4	&	a
ff

R	R	L	L	L	L	R	R	R	R	L	L
st	hl	dg	dr	st	hl	dg	dr	st	hl	dig	dr
1	&	a	2	&	a	3	&	a	4	&	a

Repeat the phrase beginning on page 61, on the other side without a pause. This requires you, once again, to suddenly become very quiet.

* Brush the right foot forward and then back, crossing to the left and in back of the right foot; put the ball of the foot down; start swiveling counterclockwise as you do a right and left heel-drop. Complete the single turn by rocking on to the heels to do right and left toe-drops. Once you get the hang of this turn, it can be done quickly and very smoothly. It is called a "Rhythm Turn."

Dynamic Play

1. Experiment with the large-scale dynamics of any combination in this book. Try to do each one gently, strongly, smoothly or percussively. Use such images as flowing water, a storm, a drunken person, a baby, different animals, to help you find varied dynamics of sound and movement.

2. Experiment with *crescendo* and *decrescendo* within any parts of combinations in the book. See how changing dynamics affects the expression and feeling of the phrase.

3. Make a phrase that contains accents. Try starting the phrase a little earlier or later, causing the accents to shift. Or, keep the starting point the same; but try accenting different parts of the step. See how that changes its rhythmic feel.

4. Listen to a variety of music works with the same instrumentation (for instance, four different piano pieces). Notice how the large-scale dynamics, including volume and quality of sound, change from piece to piece. Then focus on individual phrases. Are there dynamic nuances within the phrase?

5. Experiment dynamically with steps you have learned or made. Choose the dynamic expressions you like the best.

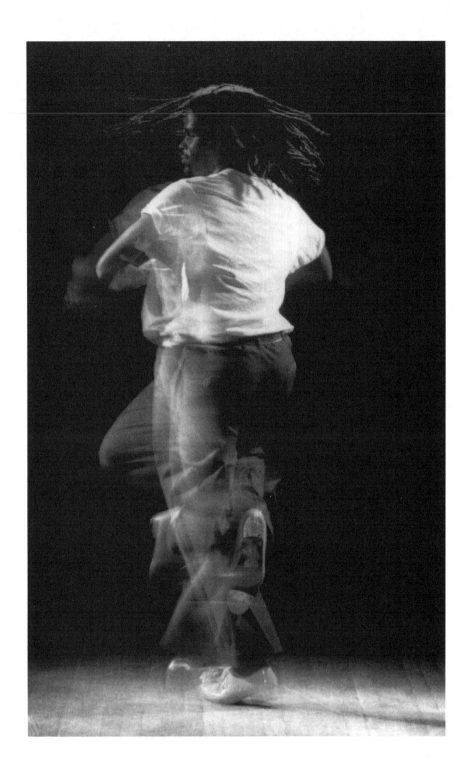

5

synCOpation

SYNCOPATION IS THE SPICE of tap dance. Accenting the beats that are expected to be unimportant adds personality to the rhythm. John Bubbles, in the early 1920s, was the first tap dancer to popularize complex syncopated rhythms with heel-drops and stomps. This style of tap dance, advanced mostly by African-American tap artists, became known as "rhythm tap."

I would not call myself a rhythm tap dancer, because not all of my rhythms have the swing of jazz; but I have been greatly influenced by rhythm tap and its marvelous syncopation. In this chapter, I will explain different types of syncopation, from the simplest to the more complex, and will give examples for each. Each combination establishes the regular metrical accent, as well as demonstrates the particular kind of syncopation in an original way. Throughout the rest of the book, almost all of the combinations are syncopated, so you will have many more examples of all kinds of syncopation. This chapter will help you understand them more fully.

Syncopating the Beat

The simplest way to syncopate is to accent on a particular beat that is not expected to be accented, as implied by the measure.

$\frac{4}{4}$ Time Signature

In $\frac{4}{4}$ time, the implied main accent is on count 1, with a lesser, implied accent on count 3. Much of swinging jazz and funk music accent the 2 and the 4 to create a syncopated beat. Following is an example of a Single Time

Step that accents the 1 and 3, followed by a syncopated Time Step variation that accents the 2 and 4. (Most traditional Time Steps begin on count 8; but this one begins on count 1.)

front			back			front			back
R	L		R	R		L	L		R
STA	hop		fl-	ap		fl-	ap		st
1	2	(&)	a	3	(&)	a	4	(&)	a
>				>					
>									

back			front			back			front		
L	L		R	L		R	R		L	L	R
br	st		STA	hop		br	st		STA	dr	hop
1	(&)	a	2	(&)	a	3	(&)	a	4	&	a
			>						>		
			>						>		

Alternates sides.

$\frac{3}{4}$ Time Signature (Waltz Clog)

In $\frac{3}{4}$ time, the implied accent is on the 1 of each measure. The following combination begins with a traditional Waltz Clog and ends with a syncopated variation, which for more advanced students is great fun turning. This is also a wonderful traveling combination.

R	L	L	L	R		L	R	R	R	L	
STO	sh-	fl*	b-	ch		STO	sh-	fl	b-	ch	
1	&	2	&	3	(&)	1	&	2	&	3	(&)
>						>					

R	L	L	L	R	R	L	L	R	L	L	L
STO	sh-	fl*	leap	st	hl	st	hl	STO	sh-	fl*	leap
1	&	2	&	3	&	1	&	2	&	3	&
>								>			

* This shuffle, called a "crossing shuffle," begins with the free foot placed slightly in back of the standing leg. It brushes to the side and then brushes in front of the standing leg. First, try the combination traveling the leaps forward slightly. Then turn the leaps and step heels clockwise, so that you accomplish two turns during the third and fourth measures.

$\frac{5}{4}$ *Time Signature*

This is an unusual, complex measure that has its major implied accent on the 1. You then have a choice of establishing a minor implied accent, either on the 3 or on the 4.

In the following combination, I set up a rhythm that has a major accent on the 1, with no minor accents. Then I make two variations. The combination consists of step heels and DIG toe-drops. When doing the DIG toe-drops, put all your weight on the heel in front of you, with the toe lifted; then drop the toe. You are literally stepping on the heel. This combination can be done as fast as a drum roll. Any variation is possible, causing different syncopations.

Perform a DIG by putting all of your weight on the heel.

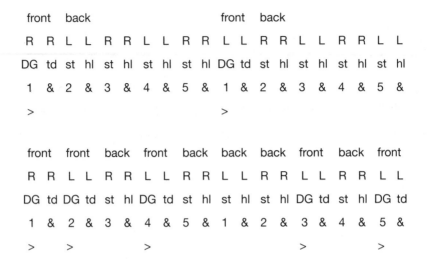

front	back									front	back								
R	R	L	L	R	R	L	L	R	R	L	L	R	R	L	L	R	R	L	L
DG	td	st	hl	st	hl	st	hl	st	hl	DG	td	st	hl	st	hl	st	hl	st	hl
1	&	2	&	3	&	4	&	5	&	1	&	2	&	3	&	4	&	5	&
>										>									

front	front	back	front	back	back	back	front	back	front
R R	L L	R R	L L	R R	L L	R R	L L	R R	L L
DG td	DG td	st hl	DG td	st hl	st hl	st hl	DG td	st hl	DG td
1 &	2 &	3 &	4 &	5 &	1 &	2 &	3 &	4 &	5 &
> >		>					>		>

Does not alternate sides.

Accenting in Between the Beats

Another more sophisticated syncopation occurs when you divide the beat. Rather than accent the beat, you accent chosen taps between the beats. The actual beat can be either silent or unaccented.

Duple Division

The following step can travel in any direction all around the room and can be done like a run. You will need to bring your weight down—or, in jazz slang—"get down" on the accents.

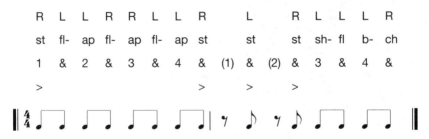

R	L	L	R	R	L	L	R		L		R	L	L	L	R
st	fl-	ap	fl-	ap	fl-	ap	st		st		st	sh-	fl	b-	ch
1	&	2	&	3	&	4	&	(1)	&	(2)	&	3	&	4	&
>						>		>		>					

Alternates sides. Perform one time or three times and continue:

L	R	R	L		R		L		R	L	L	L	R	R	R
st	fl-	ap	st		st		st		st	sh-	fl	st	sh-	fl	st
1	&	2	&	(3)	&	(4)	&	(1)	&	2	&	3	&	4	&
>			>		>		>		>			>			>
							>		>			>			

Perform one time. The entire combination alternates sides.

Triplet Division

R		L	L		R	R		L	L		R
chug		fl-	ap		fl-	ap		fl-	ap		STA
1	(&)	a	2	(&)	a	3	(&)	a	4	(&)	a
>									>		

		R			L	L		L	R		R
		STO			fl-	ap		hl	dig		dr
(1)	(&)	a	(2)	(&)	a	3	(&)	a	4	(&)	a
		>							>		
		>									

L		R	R		R	R		L			L
hl		sh-	fl		st	hl		STA			STO
1	(&)	a	2	(&)	a	3	(&)	a	(4)	(&)	a
>								>			>
											>

		R	R	R	L	L	R	L	L	L	L
		fl-	ap	hl	dig	dr	hl	sh-	fl	st	hl
(1)	(&)	a	2	&	a	3	&	a	4	&	a
			>				>				

Does not alternate sides.

Half-Time Triplets

When you make three even sounds during two beats, you end up with a wonderfully syncopated rhythm. To get the hang of this before you try the combinations, clap the following rhythm repetitively:

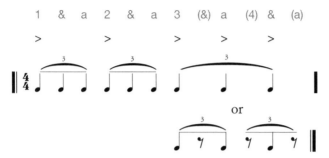

Notice how counts 3 and 4 are divided into one even, slow triplet. The resulting accents on the unexpected "a" and "&" are syncopated. When you first start doing half-time triplets, count the "a" and "&" to be sure you are really doing equally divided triplets. Once you master that, you can stop counting and just feel the slow even triplet.

Following is a traveling combination with half-time triplets:

R	L	L		R	R		L	L		R	L
chug	fl-	ap		fl-	ap		sh-	fl		hop	fl-*
1	(&)	a	2	(&)	a	3	(&)	a	4	(&)	a •
>											

*   The hop fl-ap starts on the "a" after the 4 and ends on the 1; so it is doubling the triplet. A dot, or period (.), between counts symbolizes an extra sound.

L	R	R	BOTH	R	R	L
-ap	Tip	Tip†	chug	fl-	ap	fl-
1	(&)	a	(2)	&	(a)	3	(&)	a	4	(&)	a
	>	>	>			
			>			

†   Keep these toe Tips on the floor, so that you can chug directly from it.

1	(&)	a	2	(&)	a	3	(&)	a	4	&	a
L		R	R		L	L		R	R	L	L
-ap		fl-	ap		fl-	ap		db-	le-	fl-	ap

1	(&)	a	(2)	&	(a)	3	(&)	a	(4)	&	(a)
		front‡		cr ba		front		back		back	
L		R		R		R		R		R	
hl		br		br		br		br		Tip†	
>		>		>		>		>		>	

† Keep these toe Tips on the floor, so that you can chug directly from it.

‡ You can do a counterclockwise pivot turn as you do the brushes, using the second crossing brush to get you started into the turn.

Does not alternate sides.

This combination works beautifully following the triplet combination described immediately above. It results in an interesting eight-bar traveling phrase that can end with a turn and that can be repeated over and over on the same side.

Quadruplet Division

Practice the following combination to attain faster changes of weight and shuffles, as well as work on syncopation. It travels slightly forward.

1	e	&	a	2	e	&	a	3	e	&	a	4	e	&	a
R	L	L	L	R	L	L	L	R	L	L	L	R	L	L	L
st	sh-	fl	st	st	sh-	fl	st	st	sh-	fl	st	st	sh-	fl	st
>				>				>				>			

1	e	&	a	2	e	&	a	3	e	&	a	(4)	e	(&)	a
R	L	L	L	R	R	R	L	L	L	L	L		R		L
st	sh-	fl	st	sh-	fl	st	db-	le-	sh-	fl	st		DG		st
>			>			>					>		>		>

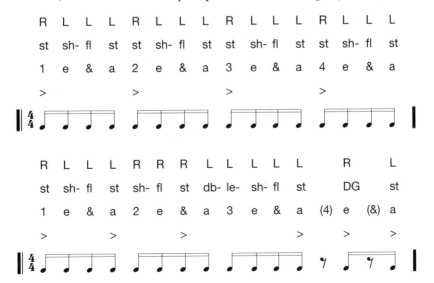

Does not alternate sides.

As a more advanced step, substitute a hop for any step to make it change sides.

Combines Duples, Triplets, and Quads with Mixed Syncopations

R		L	L	L	L	R		L		R	R	R	R
chug		dig	dr	st	hl	chug		chug		dig	dr	st	hl
1	(2)	&	3	&	4	&	(1)	&	(2)	&	3	&	4
>		>				>		>		>			
>						>		>					

cr b turning counter

L		L	R	R	L	R	R	R	L	L	R	R	R			L	L	
br		lp	3-	s-	rf*	br	st	hl	st	hl	br	st	hl			br	st	
1	2	&	a	3	&	4	&	1	&	2	&	3	(&)	a	(4)	&	(a)
>			>			>		>				>			>	>	>	
																>		

R		L	L	L	L	R		L		R	R	R	R
ch		dig	dr	st	hl	ch		ch		dig	dr	st	hl
1	(2)	&	3	&	4	&	(1)	&	(2)	&	3	&	4
>		>				>		>		>			
>						>		>					

	L		R		L	L	L	L	R	L		R
	ch		ch		dg	dr	ba	hl	hl	ch		ch
(1)	2	(3)	4	(1)	2	e	&	a	3	&	(4)	&
	>		>		>					>		>
										>		>

Alternates sides.

* **Turn to the back on the leap, counterclockwise, and continue the turn to the front during the next measure.**

Syncopation Play

1. Make new variations for each type of syncopation.

2. Choreograph syncopated combinations in different time signatures.

3. Use your musical intuition to make combinations that combine any of the types of syncopations.

4. Look at combinations throughout the book and find the syncopations.

5. Listen to jazz music selections. Concentrate on a particular instrument, and see if you hear any syncopations. What kind are they? Can you duplicate the rhythms with your feet?

6. Figure out how to do one triplet within four beats. (This is twice as slow as the half-time triplet.) Make a combination that includes these very slow quarter-time triplets.

7. Read Ted Reed's *Progressive Steps to Syncopation for the Modern Drummer* for more examples of syncopated rhythms.[1] Choose rhythms from the book to realize for your feet.

6

Fastest Feet

THROUGHOUT THE HISTORY OF TAP, dancers have competed for the "fastest feet." The audience waits for the moment when Stop-time comes in the music, and the tap dancer dazzles us with remarkable speed.[1]

How can you learn to tap faster? Honi Coles, after a largely unsuccessful engagement in New York City in 1931, went home to Philadelphia and practiced ten to sixteen hours a day. His goal was to have the "fastest feet in the business."[2]

So, we know it takes practice. But some people practice and still reach an impasse. What can you do, technically, to overcome that impasse?

In this chapter, I notate certain steps that lend themselves to the possibility of speed over at least sixteen measures. Most of these combinations have no rests. Instead, they have a continuous string of sounds much like the scales that a pianist practices to gain facile fingers. The importance of practicing even rhythmic steps without rests is that you are forced to learn to make invisible, lightning-quick weight changes.

The chapter is divided into four sections: Shuffles, Paddle and Rolls, Crawls, and Riffs. First, the basic step is described with technical tips about the weight changes and use of the leg which are the two most important aspects of attaining speed. Second, I suggest progressively more difficult combinations using the basic step.

You should practice each short combination independently. It is vital that you repeat each combination without pause, because the transition from the end back to the beginning is always important. To increase your speed progressively, use a metronome, drum machine, variable-speed cassette player, or faster and faster selections of music.

Listen carefully to your dancing. Do not forfeit the musicality of the combinations for speed. It is important that your dancing not only be rhythmically even, but that it also clearly articulate the accents and has a sense of phrasing. In order to tell how musical and accurate your feet are, record your dancing and then listen to it.

When you have memorized the short combinations and have reached a fast pace, start putting the combinations together. At the end of each section in this chapter, I make a suggestion about combining the phrases. In addition, try combining the short phrases in your own way. The first achievement to strive for is to dance repetitions of a short, four-count phrase lightning fast. A much more sophisticated—and exciting—skill is to be able to sparkle through an extended variation.

I encourage you to devise your own combinations. Practicing your own combinations of basic steps will be just as beneficial to your dancing as practicing mine. And, you will get an added benefit: there is nothing more satisfying than making up a step you haven't seen before, struggling with it, and practicing it—and, lo and behold—it becomes easy and flowing. In addition, it is all yours. Each section ends with further suggestions about how to make your own phrases to achieve this goal.

I have given specific technical tips throughout the chapter, but there are also general principles that apply to all steps, whether the steps are yours or mine. I have found that if I make my sound while maintaining the correct balance between movement in the hip joint (where the upper leg joins the pelvis), the knee joint, and the ankle joint, I get a more resonant crisp sound, I can go very fast, and I don't get tired. Also, the faster I dance, the smaller and more relaxed I try to make the steps. This combination of balanced movement through the leg and keeping the movement small and released will result in crisp, lightning-fast tapping.

Shuffles

Placement of the Shuffles

I describe three different placements of the shuffles, each resulting in a different tone. There are other options, though; so play with your own ideas as well.

1. Place your shuffling leg right next to your standing leg, which is straight. The sound is made with the center of your toe tap and is high-pitched. This is the most difficult placement of the three to do correctly. (In order to get even a higher pitched and lighter sound, lift your shuffling hip and your weight to make the sound just with the front tip of your toe tap; this is more advanced.)

2. Place your shuffling leg opened gently to the side—not turned out. Strike the floor toward the inside of the bottom of the toe tap, and you will get a slightly deeper sound. This is the easiest placement to shuffle correctly.

3. Place your shuffling leg in back of you, with both legs very slightly turned out and slightly bent. If you make the sound with the inside edge of the toe tap, you will get a very deep sound.

Parallel closed placement of a shuffle.

Open side placement of a shuffle.

Back placement of a shuffle.

Single Shuffle

I.

R	R		R	R		R	R		R	R	
sh-	fl		sh-	fl		sh-	fl		sh-	fl	
a	1	(&)	a	2	(&)	a	3	(&)	a	4	(&)

R	R		R	R		R	R		R		
sh-	fl		sh-	fl		sh-	fl		STO		
a	1	(&)	a	2	(&)	a	3	(&)	a	(4)	(&)
									>		

Placement   Perform the exercise in each of the three placements.

Technical tips   Relax the ankle. Really let it shake out without any flexing or pointing of the foot. Bring the movement into the hip joint, creating an up-and-down movement of the leg, as though you were a marionette with a string attached to the knee. Let the lower part of the leg hang. As the knee comes up, do not bring the calf farther back than at a right angle to the floor. In other words, you are minimizing the active use of the knee and ankle joints—mostly using the hip joint.

Incorrect preparation for a shuffle.

Correct preparation for a shuffle.

Double Shuffle

II.

R	R	R	R			R	R	R	R		
db-	le-	sh-	fl			db-	le-	sh-	fl		
1	&	a	2	(&)	(a)	3	&	a	4	(&)	(a)

R	R	R	R		R	R		R			
db-	le-	sh-	fl		sh-	fl		STO			
1	&	a	2	(&)	a	3	(&)	a	(4)	(&)	(a)
								>			

Placement   Use all three placements.

Technical tips   In a double shuffle, the foot stays near the floor through the two shuffles. Then the leg is drawn up from the hip joint at the end of each double shuffle. The less forward and back movement you have during the two shuffles and the drawing up of the leg, the better. If you hear a scrape instead of a crisp light sound, you probably have too much forward-back movement. As with the single shuffle, keep the ankle and lower leg passive and relaxed. You may find that the foot does a circular movement (the right foot goes counterclockwise, the left foot goes clockwise) as you relax the ankle and lower leg and minimize the forward-backward movement. Discovering this very small circle in the double shuffles and in the following shuffle-strings will help you gain speed and get a crispness to the sound. Rhythmically, double shuffles usually start on the downbeat and single shuffles start on the upbeat.

double shuffle:	1 & a 2
two single shuffles:	a 1 (&) a 2

Shuffle String

III.

R	R	R	R	R	R	R	R	R	R
sh-	fl-	sh-	fl-	sh-	fl-	sh-	fl	st	hl
1	&	a	2	&	a	3	&	a	4

Alternates sides.

Placement   Use all three placements.

Technical tips   The same tips apply here as for the double shuffle. The shuffles should be as small as possible with little forward-back movement, easy-moving hip joint, and later, as you get more relaxed, a slight circle of the ankle that comes from letting, not pushing, the circle to happen.

IV.

R	R	R	R	R	R	R	R	R	R	R	R
sh-	fl-	sh-	fl-	sh-	fl-	sh-	fl-	sh-	fl-	sh-	fl
1	&	a	2	&	a	3	&	a	4	&	a
>						>					

R	R	R	R	R	R	R	R	R	R
sh-	fl-	sh-	fl-	sh-	fl-	sh-	fl	st	hl
1	&	a	2	&	a	3	&	a	4	(&)	(a)
>						>				

Alternates sides.

Placement

a.   Use all three placements, one at a time.
b.   Counts 1 & a 2 & a: placement 1
     Counts 3 & a 4 & a: placement 2
     Second measure, counts 1 & a 2 & a 3 &:   placement 3
c.   Reverse
d.   Circle smoothly from the 1st placement to the 2nd to the 3rd throughout the combination. Be sure to hear your tone gradually go from high and light to low and heavy.
e.   Reverse
f.   First measure, circle from front to back; second measure, circle from back to front.
g.   Reverse

V.

R	R	R	R	R	R	R	R	R	R	R	R
sh-	fl-	sh-	fl-	sh-	fl-	sh-	fl-	sh-	fl-	sh-	fl
1	&	a	2	&	a	3	&	a	4	&	a
>						>					

R	R	R	R	R	R	R	R	R	R	R	R
sh-	fl-	sh-	fl-	sh-	fl-	sh-	fl-	sh-	fl	st	hl
1	&	a	2	&	a	3	&	a	4	&	a
>						>					

Alternates sides.

Placement   Same as for previous exercise.

Technical tips   When you repeat the exercise, transfer the weight immediately as you step, so that there is no pause from the end of the exercise to the beginning of the repetition. Don't wait for the heel-drop to transfer your weight.

SINGLES SHUFFLES, DOUBLE SHUFFLES, AND SHUFFLE STRINGS COMBINED

VI.

R	L	L	L	R	R	R	L	L	L	R	R
st	sh-	fl	st	sh-	fl	st	sh-	fl	st	sh-	fl
1	&	a	2	&	a	3	&	a	4	&	a
>			>			>			>		

R	L	L	L	L	L	R	R	R	R	R	L
st	db-	le-	sh-	fl	st	db-	le-	sh-	fl	st	sh-
1	&	a	2	&	a	3	&	a	4	&	a
>						>			>		

L	L	L	L	L	L	L	L	R	R	R	R
-fl-	sh-	fl-	sh-	fl-	sh-	fl-	st-	sh-	fl-	sh-	fl-
1	&	a	2	&	a	3	&	a	4	&	a
							>				

R	R	R	R	R	L	L	L	L	L
-sh-	fl-	sh-	fl	st	db-	le-	sh-	fl	st
1	&	a	2	&	a	3	&	a	4	(&)	(a)
			>						>		

Does not alternate sides.

Placement   First, do the shuffles to the sides (direction 2). When that becomes very comfortable, practice placements 1 and 3.

Technical Tip   As you get faster, your steps should become like runs, with easily rebounding knees. You can make the combination change sides by adding a step at the end of the combination on the "a" after the 4.

SHUFFLES AND HEEL-DROPS AND TOE-DROPS

VII.

↑	↙	←	↗	↓	→	↑	↓	↑	↙	←	↗	↓	→
R	R	L	R	R	L	R	R	R	R	L	R	R	L	R	R
sh-	fl	hl	sh-	fl	hl	db-	le-	sh-	fl	hl	sh-	fl	hl	st	hl
1	e	&	a	2	e	&	a	3	e	&	a	4	e	&	a
	>				>				>				>		

Alternates sides.

Technical tips   When doing a heel-drop, don't let your body go up and down. Instead, relax the standing knee so that it bends slightly and moves forward as you do the heel-drop. Make the lift of the heel prior to the heel-drop as small as possible. Think only of the "down," not of the "up." If you follow this advice, you will produce a louder, deeper heel sound. Some tap dancers speak of their shoes as drum sets, with their heels performing like a bass drum.

When you have perfected this variation, learn it with the standing-leg heel-drops going right and left according to the arrows. Moving the heels right and left will cause the standing leg to rotate out and in. The direction of the arrow matches the direction your heel would move, looking down on your foot as you dance. You can also perform the shuffles so that they cross front with a turn-out, and then come back to parallel. Follow the arrows for the shuffles. This step looks much fancier.

VIII.

The following step is the same as the one above, except that we will substitute toe-drops for some of the heel-drops. This will cause the step to travel to the left.

↑	↙	←	↗	↓	←	↑	↓	↑	↙	←	↗	↓	←		
R	R	L	R	R	L	R	R	R	R	L	R	R	L	R	R
sh-	fl	hl	sh-	fl	td	db-	le-	sh-	fl	hl	sh-	fl	td	st	hl
1	e	&	a	2	e	&	a	3	e	&	a	4	e	&	a
		>			>					>			>		

Alternates sides.

Technical tips This step requires excellent balance, especially to be able to accent the toe-drops. First, try it with parallel shuffles, then add the crossing shuffles according to the arrows. The arrows refer to the direction of the movement of the shuffles as you look down at your shuffling foot.

SHUFFLE COMBO

Exercise I	R side;	2 measures
	L side;	2 measures
Exercise II	R side;	2 measures
	L side;	2 measures
Exercise III	R side;	1 measure
	L side;	1 measure
Exercise IV	R side;	2 measures
Exercise VI	L side;	4 measures

Alternates sides.

Shuffle Play

1. Try shuffles in additional possible positions—including crossing, turned out, and turned parallel in all directions.
2. Make new combinations with shuffles, double shuffles, shuffle strings, heel-drops, and toe-drops.
3. Try longer strings of shuffles without losing their musicality.

Paddle and Roll

Basic Paddle and Roll

R	L	L	L	
hl	dg	dr	st	Repeat other side without pause, etc.
1	e	&	a	
>				

R	R	R	R	
dg	dr	st	hl	Repeat other side without pause, etc.
1	e	&	a	
>				

Technical tips   The two steps above are exactly the same except for the accent. When the accent is on the heel-drop, let a heavier use of gravity make the accent, and the dig should be light and easy. When it is on the dig, strike the floor harder, again letting gravity help you. In order to gain speed, change the weight on the step—don't wait for the heel-drop. Let the hips move easily with the legs. Just before the dig, peel the foot off the floor from heel to toe, let the dig fall, hitting the floor from back to front. (Always do a dig with a bent knee from back to front. If you go straight down with a straight knee, you will gouge the floor and make a less resonant sound.) You do not need to lift the legs higher than necessary, or flex the feet more than necessary. This step uses all three joints equally—hip, knee, and ankle. Keep them all released and moving only as much as necessary, and you will have an easy Paddle and Roll that can be as fast as a machine gun. In fact, an alternate name for this step is the "Tommy Gun."[3]

Incorrect dig.   *Correct dig.*

I.

Basic Paddle and Roll Exercise with Two Shifting Accents

R	L	L	L	L	R	R	R	R	L	L	L	L	R	R	R
hl	dg	dr	st	hl	dg	dr	st	hl	dg	dr	st	hl	dg	dr	st
1	e	&	a	2	e	&	a	3	e	&	a	4	e	&	a
>				>				>				>			

R	L	L	L	L	R	R	R	R	L	L	L	L		L	
hl	dg	dr	st	hl	dg	dr	st	hl	dg	dr	st	hl		hl	
1	e	&	a	2	e	&	a	3	e	&	a	4	(e)	&	(a)
>				>				>				>		>	

R	R	R	R	L	L	L	L	R	R	R	R	L	L	L	L
dg	dr	st	hl	dg	dr	st	hl	dg	dr	st	hl	dg	dr	st	hl
1	e	&	a	2	e	&	a	3	e	&	a	4	e	&	a
>				>				>				>			

R	R	R	R	L	L	L	L	R	R	R	R	L	L	R	L
dg	dr	st	hl	dg	dr	st	hl	dg	dr	st	hl	dg	dr	hl	st
1	e	&	a	2	e	&	a	3	e	&	a	4	e	&	a
>				>				>				>		>	

Alternates sides.

Technical tips Follow the tips for the basic Paddle and Roll. When doing heel-drops on a standing leg (as in counts "4 &" in the second measure, and count "&" after the 4 in the final measure), lift the heel only as much as necessary. Think only of the down, not the up. The standing leg should have a relaxed knee that goes forward and back to its original position as you heel-drop, rather than the entire body going up and down.

II.

Paddle and Roll with Four Shifting Accents

For a more complicated drill that shifts accents four times, refer to the drills in Chapter 4, under the heading "Accents."

III.

Double Paddle and Roll

R	L	L	L	L	R	R	R	R	L	L	L	L	R	R	R
hl	dg	dr	st	hl	dg	dr	st	hl	dg	dr	st	hl	dg	dr	dg
1	e	&	a	2	e	&	a	3	e	&	a	4	e	&	a
>				>				>				>			

R	R	R	L	L	L	L	R	R	R	R	R	R	L	L	L
dr	st	hl	dg	dr	st	hl	dg	dr	dg	dr	st	hl	dg	dr	st
1	e	&	a	2	e	&	a	3	e	&	a	4	e	&	a
	>				>							>			

Alternates sides.

IV.

ANOTHER EXAMPLE OF DOUBLE PADDLE AND ROLL EXERCISE

R	L	L	L	L	R	R	R	R	L	L	L	L	L	L	R
hl	dg	dr	st	hl	dg	dr	st	hl	dg	dr	dg	dr	st	hl	dg
1	e	&	a	2	e	&	a	3	e	&	a	4	e	&	a
>				>				>						>	

R	R	R	R	R	L	L	L	L	L	L	R	R	R	R	R
dr	dg	dr	st	hl	dg	dr	dg	dr	st	hl	dg	dr	dg	dr	st
1	e	&	a	2	e	&	a	3	e	&	a	4	e	&	a
				>						>					

Does not alternate sides.

V.

ANOTHER DOUBLE PADDLE AND ROLL

The following two measures are meant to be added to exercise III or IV. If you are adding them to exercise III, start with the left heel-drop, and reverse all the feet described below.

R	L	L	L	L	L	L	R	R	R	R	R	R	L	L	L
hl	dg	dr	dg	dr	st	hl	dg	dr	dg	dr	st	hl	dg	dr	dg
1	e	&	a	2	e	&	a	3	e	&	a	4	e	&	a
>						>						>			

L	L	L	R	R	R	R	R	R	L	L	L	L	L	L	
dr	st	hl	dg	dr	dg	dr	st	hl	dg	dr	dg	dr	st	hl	
1	e	&	a	2	e	&	a	3	e	&	a	4	e	&	(a)
		>						>						>	

Technical tips   For doubles or triples (or more), try to balance the up-and-down movement of the ankle flexing, and the forward and back movement made by the knee and hip joint. Either one by itself is less efficient. Keep the movement small, and do the dig draws slightly in front of the standing leg. Don't flex the ankle any more than necessary. See how a slight, easy supportive movement of the hip can help increase your speed.

VI.

TRIPLE PADDLE AND ROLL

R	L	L	L	L	R	R	R	R	L	L	L	L	L	L	L
hl	dg	dr	st	hl	dg	dr	st	hl	dg	dr	dg	dr	dg	dr	st
1	e	&	a	2	e	&	a	3	e	&	a	4	e	&	a
>				>				>							

L	R	R	L	L	L	L	L	L	L	L	R	R	(L	L	L)
hl	st	hl	dg	dr	dg	dr	dg	dr	st	hl	st	hl	(dg	dr	st)
1	e	&	a	2	e	&	a	3	e	&	a	4	(e	&	a)
>	>									>		>			
	>											>			

Alternates sides.

Technical tip   First, practice this step, ending on count "4." Once you are comfortable with that, add the sounds in parentheses.

VIIa.

SHIFTING ACCENT COMBINATIONS

	→ ←			← →											
	open			closed											
R	R	L	R	R	L	R	R	L	L	L	L	R	R	R	R
ba	hl	hl	ba	hl	hl	st	hl	dg	dr	st	hl	dg	dr	st	hl
1	e	&	a	2	e	&	a	3	e	&	a	4	e	&	a
>		>		>		>		>				>			

Alternates sides.

VIIb.

```
        ← →        → ←
        open       closed
R   L   L   R   L   L   R   L   L   R   R   R   R           R
hl  ba  hl  hl  ba  hl  hl  st  hl  dg  dr  st  hl          hl
1   e   &   a   2   e   &   a   3   e   &   a   4  (e)  &  (a)
>   >           >               >   >                   >           >
    >           >                                           >
```

Does not alternate sides.

VIIc.

```
        ← →        → ←
        open       closed
R   L   L   R   L   L   R   L   L   R   R   R   R   L   L   L
hl  ba  hl  hl  ba  hl  hl  st  hl  dg  dr  st  hl  dg  dr  st
1   e   &   a   2   e   &   a   3   e   &   a   4   e   &   a
>   >           >               >   >                   >
    >
```

Alternates sides.

VIId.

```
        ← →        → ←
        open       closed
R   L   L   R   L   L   R   L   L   R   R   R   R   L   L   R
hl  ba  hl  hl  ba  hl  hl  st  hl  dg  dr  st  hl  dg  dr  hl
1   e   &   a   2   e   &   a   3   e   &   a   4   e   &   a
>   >           >               >   >                   >           >
```

Does not alternate sides.

The final variation above is the most difficult because, in order to repeat it, you must perform two quick heel-drops in a row. This skill is necessary in the following combinations.

1. Practice VIIa, VIIb, VIIc, and VIId, separately and repetitively.
2. Practice three repetitions of VIIa, followed by one repetition of VIIb. Repeat on the other side.
3. Practice four repetitions of VIIa, three repetitions of VIIc, and then one of VIIb. Repeat on the other side.
4. Practice four repetitions of VIIa, three repetitions of VIIc, followed by one of VIId. Repeat on the other side.

Technical tips   Once you can do all the above variations, look at the arrows, which refer to the direction in which the heel moves during the heel-drops. As the right heel moves slightly to the right, the right leg rotates inward; as the right heel moves to the left, the right leg rotates outward. This makes the step more visually magical, giving it the pigeon-toed, rubber-legged look of the Charleston.

PADDLE COMBO

III   Starts with right heel; 2 measures
IV   Starts with left heel; 2 measures
V   Starts with left heel; 2 measures
VI   (Without step in parentheses), starts with right heel; 2 measures
VIIa   Four times, starts with ball of left foot; 4 measures
VIIc   Three times, starts with right heel; 3 measures
VIIb   One time, starts with left heel; 1 measure

Alternates sides.

Paddle Play

1. Make the Paddles travel in all directions, including crossing front and back.
2. Devise new steps, combining "st hl," "br st hl," Paddles, Double Paddles and Triple Paddles. Innumerable combinations are possible. Be sure the accents are clear and interesting to you.
3. Choreograph combinations using four or more "dig dr" in a row, combined with the other types of Paddle and Roll.

4. Make combinations that use the Paddle and Rolls in triplet divisions of the beat. This will result in shifting accents.

The Crawl

The Crawl is a traveling step that skims across the floor with toe-drops and heel-drops that turn the leg in and out without lifting the leg off the floor.

The One-Legged Crawl

The following four combinations travel to the right. That means that the toe-drops turn the right leg out, and the heel-drops turn the right leg in, so that they take you to the right. Arrows are included to be sure you understand the directions.

I.

	→	→	→	→			
R	R	R	R	R			
ba	hl	td	hl	td			
1	&	2	&	3	(&	4	&)
>							

Alternates sides.

II.

	→	→	→	→	→	→			→	→	→	→		
R	R	R	R	R	L	L	L	R	R	R	R	R		
ba	hl	td	hl	td	br	st	hl	ba	hl	td	hl	td		
1	&	2	&	3	&	4	&	1	&	2	&	3	(& 4	&)
>							>							

Alternates sides.

III.

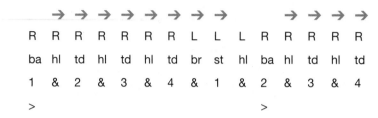

→	→	→	→	→	→	→	→		→	→	→	→
R	R	R	R	R	R	R	L	L	L	R	R	R	R	R
ba	hl	td	hl	td	hl	td	br	st	hl	ba	hl	td	hl	td
1	&	2	&	3	&	4	&	1	&	2	&	3	&	4
>										>				

Alternates sides.

IV.

→	→	→	→	→	→	→	→	→	→		→	→
R	R	R	R	R	R	R	R	R	L	L	L	R	R	R
ba	hl	td	hl	td	hl	td	hl	td	br	st	hl	ba	hl	td
1	&	2	&	3	&	4	&	1	&	2	&	3	&	4
>												>		

Alternates sides.

Technical tips   Do not put weight on the crawling foot until the final toe-drop before each brush step. On that toe-drop, transfer the weight immediately.

The Two-Legged Crawl
In the Two-Legged Crawl, the weight is placed evenly on both feet. Begin by standing on both feet. Every part of the combination travels to the left.

V.

R	L	R	L	R	L	R	L
td	td	hl	hl	td	td	hl	hl
1	&	2	&	3	&	4	&
>				>			

R	L	R	L	R	L	R	L
td	td	hl	hl	td	td	hl	hl
1	&	2	&	3	&	4	&
>				>			

toes			heels			toes	
BO	R	L	BO	R	L	BO	R
click	td	td	click	hl	hl	click	td
1	&	2	&	3	&	4	&
>			>			>	

	heels			toes			heels		
L	BO	R	L	BO	R	L	BO	R	L
td	click	hl	hl	cl	td	td	cl	hl	hl
1	&	2	&	**3**	2	3	4	5	**4**
	>			>			>		

Technical tips   The Two-Legged Crawl differs from the Cramp Roll, in that a Cramp Roll begins when you jump in the air. But with The Crawl you stay on the ground. If the toe-drops and heel-drops are equal in the distance they travel, you will travel in a straight line. If the toe-drops are bigger, you will travel in a circle. Try it both ways—in a straight line and in a circle. Keep the hip joints and knee joints loose, so that the movement goes through all the joints equally.

More Two-Legged and One-Legged Crawl Combinations

VI.

This combination travels to the left on the first measure and to the right on the second measure. Begin with your weight on two feet.

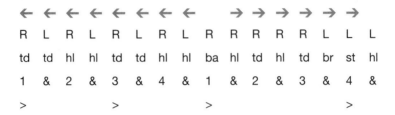

←	←	←	←	←	←	←	←	→	→	→	→	→	→		
R	L	R	L	R	L	R	L	R	R	R	R	R	L	L	L
td	td	hl	hl	td	td	hl	hl	ba	hl	td	hl	td	br	st	hl
1	&	2	&	3	&	4	&	1	&	2	&	3	&	4	&
>				>				>				>			

VII.

The following combination travels to the right:

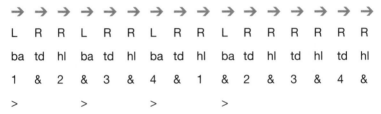

→	→	→	→	→	→	→	→	→	→	→	→	→	→	→	→
L	R	R	L	R	R	L	R	R	L	R	R	R	R	R	R
ba	td	hl	ba	td	hl	ba	td	hl	ba	td	hl	td	hl	td	hl
1	&	2	&	3	&	4	&	1	&	2	&	3	&	4	&
>			>			>			>						

Does not alternate sides.

Technical tip   After each ball-tap, keep the left foot on the floor as the other foot crawls. There is little weight on the right crawling foot until the very last heel-drop.

VIII.

The following combination travels in the direction of the arrows:

→	→	→	→	→	→	→	→	→	←	←	←	←	→	→	
L	R	R	L	R	R	R	L	R	L	R	L	L	R	R	L
ba	td	hl	ba	td	hl	td	hl	hl	hl	ba	td	hl	st	hl	dr
1	&	2	&	3	&	4	&	1	&	2	&	3	&	4	&
>			>					>				>			

Does not alternate sides.

Crawl Combo

V   One time; right side; 4 measures; dynamics: quietly

VI   Three times; right side; 6 measures; dynamics: crescendo gradually through the three repetitions

II   Two times; right side, then left side; 2 measures; dynamics: loudly on the first, quietly on the second

III   One time; right side; 2 measures; dynamics: a little louder

IV   One time; left side; 2 measures; dynamics: loudest

Can alternate sides.

Crawl Play

1.   A more advanced way to do a One-Legged Crawl is to have all your weight on the crawling foot. Try it!

2.   Do Two-Legged Crawls that open the feet as far as possible and then close them. Choreograph a combination that includes the feet opening, closing and traveling to the sides.

Riffs

A Riff begins with the ball of the foot tapped directly next to the other foot, followed by a scuff. Do not lift the leg between the ball and the scuff. A reverse riff is a dig with the heel followed by a draw back, again without lifting the foot off the floor until the end of the riff.

Riffs are wonderful steps to make very fast sounds, while appearing like you are just walking.

The following riffs will be covered in this section: 3-sound; 4-sound; 5-sound; 7-sound; riffle; and the reverse of all of them.

3-SOUND RIFF (3-S-RF)

R	R	L
ba	sc	hl

Technical tips   While scuffing, swing the leg all the way to a straight position. When doing the heel-drop, don't go up and down; instead, let the standing knee bend forward and back to the original relaxed position.

4-SOUND RIFF (4-S-RF)

R	R	R	R
ba	sc	DG	td

Technical tips   Usually, when you dig with the heel, you should bend the knee and attack the sound from back to front. In this step, however, the leg is already straight from the scuff. Keeping that straight position, bring the leg down into the DIG and put some weight onto it, finishing the change of weight as you toe-drop.

5-SOUND RIFF (5-S-RF)

R	R	L	R	R
ba	sc	hl	DG	td

Technical tips   This (and all the riffs) should look and feel like an easy walk. Keep the heel-drops small, and swing the leg out straight. After you do the right side, you need to instantly change your weight on the toe-drop and quickly bring the other foot right next to the standing leg to start the left side.

7-SOUND RIFF (7-S-RF)

R	R	L	R	R	L	R
ba	sc	hl	dg	td	hl	hl

Technical tips   As you do the final heel-drop, shift your weight to the right foot.

RIFFLE (RFL)

R	R	R
ba	dg	dr

Technical tips   The dig in a riffle is a scuff that doesn't come off the floor. From the ball-tap, slide the foot directly forward into the dig. The drawback is similar to the end of a shuffle, in that you should lift the knee, rather than isolate the movement in the ankle.

All the riffs above can be reversed so that they travel backward.

3-SOUND REVERSE RIFF (3-S-R-RF)

R	R	L
dg	dr	hl

4-SOUND REVERSE RIFF F(4-S-R-RF)

R	R	R	R
dg	dr	st	hl

You may have noticed that the 4-s-r-rf is the same as a Paddle and Roll.

5-SOUND REVERSE RIFF (5-S-R-RF)

R	R	L	R	R
dg	dr	hl	st	hl

7-SOUND REVERSE RIFF (7-S-R-RF)

R	R	L	R	R	L	R
dg	dr	hl	st	hl	hl	hl

REVERSE RIFFLE (R-RFL)

R	R	R
dig	dr	sc

Once you can do all these riffs, start working on the following combinations. I will refer to each riff by name and will tell you which foot makes each sound.

Duple Division Drills

I.

R	R	L	R	R		L	L	R	L	L		R	L
5-s-rf						5-s-rf						STO	STO
1	&	2	&	3	(&)	4	&	1	&	2		3	4
			>						>			>	>
												>	>

				cross	ba										
R	R	L	R	R	L	L	L	R	R	L	R	R	L	R	R
5-s-rf	....			br	st	h	3-s-rf			3-s-r-rf			st	hl
1	&	2	&	3	&	4	&	1	&	2	&	3	&	4	&
				>				>							

Alternates sides.

Technical tips The third and fourth measures are the most difficult, because there is no extra time for the weight shifts. To gain speed, in the third measure be sure to transfer your weight on count "&" after the "2" (the DIG) and in the fourth measure on count "4" (the step). The 3-s-rf and 3-s-r-rf should be done while circling the right leg in a wide clockwise direction.

II.

open pos

R	R	R	L	R	R	L	R	R	R	L	L	R	L	L	R	L
rfl	....		hl	5-	s-	rf	....		5-	s-	rf	....		dr	hl
1	&	2	&	3	&	4	&	1	&	2	&	3	&	4	&
								>				>			

Does not alternate sides.

Technical tips Once again, and in all of the following steps, you must make the weight changes at the earliest possible moment, in order to keep the rhythm even and gain speed.

III.

open pos

R	R	L	R	R	L	R	R	R	L	L	L	R	R	R	R
rfl	....		hl	5-s-rf	....				br	st	hl	4-s-rf
1	&	2	&	3	&	4	&	1	&	2	&	3	&	4	&
						>								>	

Alternates sides.

Duple Division Riff Combo

  I   Two times; right side, then left side: eight measures.

  II   One time; right side: two measures.

 III One time; right side: two measures.

  II   One time; left side: two measures.

 III One time; left side; two measures.

Does not alternate sides.

Advanced Riff Steps in Varied Divisions of the Beat

I. DUPLE AND TRIPLET DIVISIONS

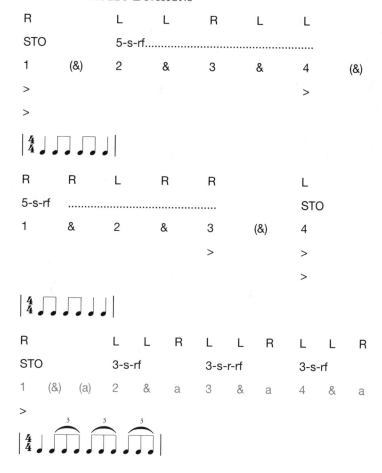

L	L	R	L	L	R	L	L	R	L		
3–s–r–rf			7–s–rf								
1	&	a	2	&	a	3	&	a	4	(&)	(a)

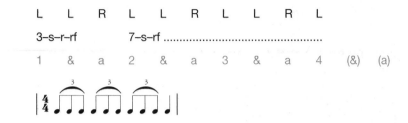

Technical tips   During the riffles and reverse riffles, first try crossing and uncrossing the riffling foot with the standing foot in your own way. Then try circling counterclockwise, one circle per 3-s-rf and 3-s-r-rf. Next, try a combination of one circle and one cross.

II. Triplet Division

R	R	L	R	R	L	R	L	L	R	L	L
7–s–rf...						3–s–r–rf			5–s–rf		
1	&	a	2	&	a	3	&	a	4	&	a
>											

R	L	L	R	R	L	L	R	L	L		R
....		br	st	5–s–rf							lp
1	&	a	2	&	a	3	&	a	4	(&)	a
			>	>					>		

Alternates sides.

Technical tips   The brush step in the second measure should be done almost like a leap, with the right leg coming directly toward the left leg and replacing it. The ending leap also replaces the left leg.

III. Quintuplet, Quadruplet, and Triplet Division

This combination is quite advanced. It is a short excerpt from one of my dances titled "Takeoff."[4]

R		L	R	R	L	R	R		R	L	L	R
STO		lp	5–s–rf						hop 5	–	s	–
1		2	2	3	4	5	3		4	e	&	a
>					>							

*ANITA FELDMAN
TAP. Anita Feldman and
Gary Schall in "Takeoff,"
by Feldman and Schall.
Photo by Tom Caravaglia.*

L	L	R	R	R	L	L	R	L	L	R	L
– rf.....		br	st	hl	5–s–rf......................					dr	hl
1	&	a	2	&	a	3	&	a	4	&	a
>			>						>		

R			L	R	R	L	R	R	L	L	L	R
STO			lp	5–s–rf.....................br			st	hl	3–			
1			2	e	&	a	3	&	a	4	&	a
>						>						
>												

R	L	R	R	L	R	R	L	L	L	L	R
s–rf		3–s–r–rf			st	hl	dig	dr	ba	hl	hl
1	&	a	2	&	a	3	&	a	4	&	a

Alternates sides.

Advanced Riff Combo

I   One time; 4 measures.

II   Two times; right side and left side (on left side, leave out the ending leap); 4 measures.

III   Two times; left side, then right side; 8 measures.

The Advanced Riff Combo feels like it's getting wilder and faster. That is because the beat is divided into smaller divisions as the combination proceeds.

Riff Play

1. Try the combinations, reversing all the riffs and riffles.

2. Make up your own six- and eight-sound riffs. Use them in your combinations.

3. Make up other combinations using any divisions of the beats with any variety of riffs and riffles.

Fast Feet Play

Your next step is to combine shuffles, Paddles and Rolls, crawls, and riffs into your own exciting, original fast drills and combinations. Have fun! And don't forget the dynamics!

Have you made it through this entire chapter? Congratulations! Even if you think it is impossible, go back to the beginning and see if you can increase your speed further. It is amazing what practice can do!

At this point you may be asking, "How fast is 'fast'?" I have found that intermediate dancers should be able to dance at a speed of 120, when dividing each beat into four sounds. (A speed of 120 means that there are 120 beats per minute. However, since you are tapping four sounds per beat, you are actually tapping 480 notes per minute.) Advanced dancers can go as fast as 170. The longer you can hold a tempo, the more advanced you are.

As I have already mentioned, speed alone does not an artist make. Strive to go faster, but do not leave your musicality behind.

7

Traditional Tap: The Shim Sham Shimmy and Time Steps

THERE ARE SO MANY TAP TRADITIONS, but the two most important are the Shim Sham Shimmy and Time Steps.

The Shim Sham Shimmy

Go to any traditional tap dance concert, and at the end of the concert the performers will invite tappers from the audience to join them on stage for the Shim Sham Shimmy. You will see dancers of all ages, races, and levels happily dancing together. The main roots of tap are from Africa and Ireland, where dance was a participatory community event, not a performance art for the talented few. The Shim Sham Shimmy finale celebrates those roots.

But who made the Shim Sham Shimmy? In the 1920s, Leonard Reed and his partner, Willie Bryant, were touring in the American South with the Whitman Sisters troupe. They put together a dance from existing steps which they called "Goofus." Reed and Bryant intentionally made the dance easy and goofy so that members of the audience would feel comfortable joining them on stage. A boy in the show named Billy moved to New York, formed a dance trio called "Three Little Words," and started to perform

"Goofus" at the Shim Sham Club. They added a shaking of the shoulders to it and changed the name to Shim Sham Shimmy.[1] It really caught on.

Joe Jones, part of "Three Little Words," reminisced about their performances at Connie's Inn, in Harlem, in 1932: "We'd close the show at Connie's doing the Shim Sham and inviting everybody to get aboard. The whole club would join us, including the waiters. For a while, people were doing the Shim Sham up and down Seventh Avenue all night long."[2]

Ia.

THE SHIM SHAM

R	R	R		L	L	L		R	R	R	L	R	R	R
sh–	fl	st		sh–	fl	st		sh–	fl	ba–	ch	sh–	fl	st
4	&	1		2	&	3		4	&	1	&	2	&	3

Alternates sides. Repeat right side and left side.

R	R	R		L	L	L		R	R	R	L	R	R	R
sh–	fl	st		sh–	fl	st		sh–	fl	ba–	ch	sh–	fl	ba
4	&	1		2	&	3		4	&	1	&	2	&	3

One time.

Ib.

THE SHIM SHAM BREAK

	tog	to the back	left diag				apart	tog
R	L	L	L	R	R	L	R	L
STO	ba	st	hl	st	hl	st	STO	STO
4	1	2	3	&	(4)	&	1	2	3

II.

THE CROSS-OVER

				to right	cr		fr	
R	L	R	L	R	R	L	L	R
STO	st	STO	st	st	hl	st	hl	st
4	1	2	3	4	1	&	(2)	&	3

Alternates sides. Repeat right side, left side, and right side.

to left		cr	fr		
L	L	R		R	L
st	hl	st		hl	st
4	1	&	(2)	&	3

to right		cr	fr		
R	R	L		L	R
st	hl	st		hl	ba
4	1	&	(2)	&	3

III. THE TACK ANNIE

apart			tog		apart		tog		apart		tog		apart		tog	
R	L		R	R	R		L	L	L		R	R	R		L	L
STO	STO		dr	ba	STO		dr	ba	STO		dr	ba	STO		dr	st
a	4	(&)	a	1	2	(&)	a	3	4	(&)	a	1	2	(&)	a	3

Does not alternate sides. Repeat three times.

Then perform The Shim Sham Break (step Ib).

IV. Some people call the following step the "Half Break," while others call it "Falling Off a Log."

R		L	R	R	R	L
STO		st	sh–	fl	ba–	ch
4		1	&	2	&	3

Two times on the same side.

Technical tips   Face diagonally left. Fall onto the right Stomp, with the left leg extended back on a left diagonal. Then almost leap onto the next step as you change your facing to the diagonal right. Repeat.

For an extra challenge, the Half Break step can be done with an Over-the-Top.[3] On count 3, dig the outside of the toe in front of the right foot, with a deep plie on the right leg. Then, count 4 is the landing from the Over-the- Top on the right, as well as the beginning of the next repetition.

Then perform the Shim Sham Break.

Do the entire combination twice (two times of the Half Break and one time of the Break).

Falling onto the right Stomp in the Half Break.

The preceding four steps of the Shim Sham Shimmy are usually performed at the end of tap concerts. Most often, everyone does the routine once through. Just to see who is really on the ball, everyone does the Shim Sham Shimmy again; but now, whenever it is time for the Break, they remain perfectly still. There are always some who forget and find themselves doing the Break in an unintentional solo, which results in some good-natured ribbing.

Now you are ready to join in the next time the professionals beckon you from the stage.

There are three additional steps to the Shim Sham Shimmy that tappers often tag on (the fourth is a repeat of the Half Break and Shim Sham Break with an ending tagged on), but I have rarely seen them done on stage. They are a lot of fun with plenty of syncopation; they include the Suzie Q and the Jazz Step.[4]

V.

					feet tog			heels		heels	
L	R	R	R		L	R		BOTH		BOTH	
ho	sh–fl	ba	–		ch	st		cl		cl	
4	&	a	1		2	3	(4)	1	(2)	&	(3)
										>	

Repeat three times on the same side.

	heels		heels				heels		heels		
	BOTH		BOTH				BOTH		BOTH		
	cl		cl				cl		cl		
(4)	1	(2)	&	(3)	(4)		1	(2)	&	(3)	
			>						>		

VIa.

THE SUZIE Q

										↙	
L		R	R	L		R	R	L		R	R
hl		ba	DG	st		ba	DG	st		ba	DG
4	(&)	a	1	2	(&)	a	3	4	(&)	a	1

(continued)

L		R	R	L		R	R
st		dr	st				
2	(&)	a	3				

Alternates sides. Repeat two times.

Technical tips The "ba DG" is almost like the beginning of a riffle. The right ball slides directly into the DIG, with the right foot in front of the left; meanwhile, the right leg rotates from turned-in to turned-out. Your weight stays on the heel as you step to the left side with the left foot. Eight counts travel to the left. The draw is done in the direction of the arrow, crossing the left foot. This forces the left foot to circle around to the front to begin on the other side as you do the heel-drop. This step is often done with the hands clasped and the hips circling.

VIb.

The Suzie Q Break

				↙								↘			
L		R	R	L		R	R	R		L	L	R		L	L
hl		ba	DG	st		dr	st	hl		ba	DG	st		dr	st
4	(&)	a	1	2	(&)	a	3	4	(&)	a	1	2	(&)	a	3

Perform the Suzie Q Break once, then repeat the Suzie Q once more.

VII.

Jazz Step

L		L	R	L		L	R	L		L	R	L		L	R
kick		ba	tog	kick		ba	tog	kick		ba	tog	kick		ba	tog
clap		lp	st	clap		lp	st	clap		lp	st	clap		lp	st
4	(&)	a	1	2	(&)	a	3	4	(&)	a	1	2	(&)	a	3

	to front left diagonal				to front right diagonal		
R	L	L	L	L	R	R	R
hl	ba	ba	st	hl	ba	ba	st
4	1	2	3	4	1	2	3

Does not alternate sides. Repeat two times. End the last repetition with a ball-tap so that your right foot is free to continue to the next step.

Technical tips   As you clap, kick the left foot forward at the same time. Doing two things at the same time is always challenging; but, with a little practice, you'll get it. The leap is a small bouncy one that travels slightly back; and then step next to the leaping leg. On the third and fourth measures, lead the ball-taps with the hip—first with the feet and hips opening to the left, then to the right.

VIII.

Repeat step IV. Do the Half Break two times, the Shim Sham Break one time, and the Half Break two times, ending with the weight on both feet evenly. Then, for the grand finale:

RLRL	R	R	R	L	R	L
db-le-pb	br	st	hl	br	hl	STA
(4) ---1	2	3	4	1	2	3

During the br hl STA, kick the left leg, as it brushes, to the right—crossing in front of the right foot, lifting up in the center, and landing with a straight leg in front with the STA. Don't put weight on the STA, but leave it on the floor to end.

Shim Sham Play

If this dance is difficult for you, find your own way to take out some of the sounds. (For instance, on the Tack Annie, take out the draws.) If you want more of a challenge, and you can already do the dance fairly quickly, use your ingenuity to add sounds (for instance, on the Tack Annie, add a dig before any of the draws).

Time Steps

I am no longer surprised when, during guest residencies, a student says, "Oh, I know the Time Step." For some reason, it is assumed that there is only *one* Time Step. Actually, there are innumerable Time Steps; there should be at least as many Time Steps as there are tap dancers. As hoofer Jack Donohue wrote in 1929, "In the good old days every hoofer had his own Time Step by which he was recognized by the rest of his profession...."[5]

If there are so many of them, then what defines a Time Step? Time Steps originate from buck dancing, which was flat-footed close-to-the-floor dancing that combined shuffles, flaps, and steps. Bill Robinson was the first to take those steps and bring them up on the balls of the feet, which is how most Time Steps are danced today. They were originally used by dancers in the beginning of their act to set the tempo for the live musicians. The most important characteristic of the Time Step is that it is syncopated—usually with accents on the 2 and the & after the 3. It is the syncopation that makes the Time Step "speak." Traditionally, a Time Step lasts one bar and is done six times, followed by a two-bar Time Step Break. As was true in the old days, shuffles, flaps, and steps are often the main elements of the Time Step.

Most Time Steps and Time Step Breaks have standard variations, called singles, doubles, triples, triple-doubles, and triple-triples. For the first Time Step notated, I include all of the variations. I'll let you figure out the standard and your original variations for the rest.

The Buggy Ride Time Step

The Buggy Ride is the best-known Time Step. Its name comes from the way in which it is often taught, using the sentence, "And thanks for the bug-GY ride" to teach the rhythm and phrasing.[6]

There are three variations even on the basic single Time Step. They are notated below.

Single Buggy Ride Time Step

			back	front		ba	fr
	R	L	R	L	L	R	L
Var. 1	–fl	hop	st	br	st	st	sh-
Var. 2	dr	hop	st	br	st	st	dig
Var. 3	dr	hop	st	br	st	st	STA
	And	thanks	FOR	the	bug	–GY	ride
	a	1	2 (&)	a	3 (&)	a	4

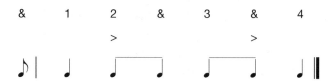

From now on, I notate only the third variation; but many of the Time Steps can be danced in any of the above three ways.

Any variation can also be performed with more of a duple than a triplet feel:

&	1	2	&	3	&	4

Jazz musicians call the duple feel "straight eighth notes," and the triplet feel "swinging or syncopated eighth notes." You can perform many of the Time

Steps either way, but be sure that you use music with a matching duple or triplet feel.

Double Buggy Ride Time Step

	a	1	(&)	a	2	(&)	a	3	(&)	a	4
							front			ba	fr
	R	L		R	R		L	L		R	L
	dr	hop		fl–	ap		br	st		st	STA
	And	thank		you	FOR		the	bug		–GY	ride
	a	1	(&)	a	2	(&)	a	3	(&)	a	4
					>					>	

Triple Buggy Ride Time Step

	a	1	&	a	2	(&)	a	3	(&)	a	4
							front			ba	fr
	R	L	R	R	R		L	L		R	L
	dr	hop	sh–	fl	st		br	st		st	STA
	And	when	will	we	TAKE		the	bug		–GY	Ride?
	a	1	&	a	2	(&)	a	3	(&)	a	4
					>					>	

Double-Triple Buggy Ride Time Step

	a	1	(&)	a	2	&	a	3	(&)	a	4
								front		ba	fr
	R	L		R	R	L	L	L		R	L
	dr	hop		fl–	ap	sh–	fl	st		st	STA
	And	thank		you	FOR	the	great	bug		–GY	ride
	a	1	(&)	a	2	&	a	3	(&)	a	4
					>					>	

TRIPLE-TRIPLE BUGGY RIDE TIME STEP

							front	ba	fr
R	L	R	R	R	L	L	L	R	L
dr	hop	sh –	fl	st	sh –	fl	st	st	STA
And	what	'll	I	DO	on	the	bug	–GY	ride?
a	1	&	a	2	&	a	3	(&) a	4
				>				>	

As you have seen, the general rule for making variations on a Time Step is adding or subtracting sounds between counts 1 and 2. To get fancier, you can change the number of sounds between counts 2 and 3. From now on, it will be up to you to play with on both the Time Steps and the Time Step Breaks. Don't hesitate to experiment. For instance, try making four or five sounds between counts 1 and 2. Or, try adding sounds between two other counts. Just keep the syncopated accent feel.

TRADITIONAL SINGLE TIME STEP BREAK
(Done after six Time Steps)

R	L		R	L	L		L	R		R	L		R	R		L	R	L
dr	hop		st	sh-	fl		st	sh-		-fl	hop		fl-	ap		ba-	ch	STA
a	1	(&)	(a) 2	(&)	a	3	(&)	a	4	(&)	a	1	(&)	a	2	(&)	a	3	4

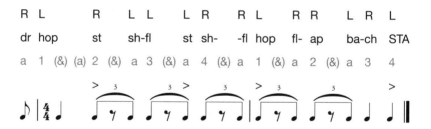

TRADITIONAL TRIPLE-TRIPLE TIME STEP BREAK
(Done after six Time Steps)

R	L	R	R	R	L	L	L		R	R
dr	hop	sh-	fl	st	sh-	fl	st		sh-	fl
a	1	&	a	2	&	a	3	(&)	a	4

									ba	front
R	L		L	R		L	L		R	L
st	sh-		-fl	hop		fl-	ap		st	STA
a	1	(&)	a	2	(&)	a	3	(&)	a	4
>				>					>	>

Traditional Half Triple Time Step Break
(Done after three Time Steps)

					front				ba	front
L	R	L	L	R		L	L		R	L
dr	hop	sh-	fl	hop		br	st		st	STO
a	1	&	a	2	(&)	a	3	(&)	a	4
	>			>					>	>

Triple-Triple Cramp Roll Time Step
(Done after three Time Steps)

R	L	R	R	R	L	L	L	R	R	L
dr	hop	sh-	fl	st	sh-	fl	st	st	hl	dig
a	1	&	a	2	&	a	3	&	a	4
	>			>				>		>

Half Time Step Break
(Done after three Time Steps)

		ba					ba			
L	R		L	R		R	L		R	L
dr	hop		st	dig		dr	hop		st	dig
a	1	(&)	a	2	(&)	a	3	(&)	a	4
				>						>

DOUBLE MANHATTAN TIME STEP
(Two bars long)

```
forward............... backward......................................... forward..................
R   L    R  L     R  R    L  L     L   R    R   L     R   R    L  L
ch  ch   ch ch    fl- ap  sh- fl   st  sh-  -fl hop   fl- ap   fl- ap
a   4 (&) a 1 (&) a 2 (&) a 3 (&) a 4 (&) a 1 (&) a 2 (&) a 3
          >            >            >
```

DOUBLE MANHATTAN TIME STEP BREAK
(Done after three Manhattan Time Steps)

```
forward............................ backward......................................... front
R   L    R  L     R  L     R  R     L  L    L   R     R   L    R   R
ch  ch   ch ch    ch ch    fl- ap   sh- fl  st  sh-   -fl hop  fl- ap
a   4 (&) a 1 (&) a 2 (&) a 3 (&) a 4 (&) a 1 (&) a 2 (&) a 3
         >  >       >              >            >
         >  >
```

TRAVELING TIME STEP
(Two bars long; duple division)

```
side          side       travel to right        turn*
R    R    R   L    L    L    R    L    R    R    L   R    R    R
sh-  fl   st  sh-  fl   ba-  ch   ba-  ch   hop* st  sh-  fl   st
4    &    1   &    2    &    3    &    4    1    2   &    3    &
     >                      >    >              >             >
```

*   **You can turn the hop in a counterclockwise direction.**

TRAVELING TIME STEP BREAK

(Done after one or three Traveling Time Steps)

				fr	ba									
L	L	R		R	L	L	R	L	L	R	L	L	R	R	R
sh-	fl	hop		hop	br	st	st	sh-	fl	hop	fl-	ap	sh-	fl	st
4	&	1		2	&	3	&	4	&	1	&	2	&	3	&
>		>				>						>			>

I have already mentioned that most Time Steps can be done with a duple or triplet feel. The Traveling Time Step works particularly well with a duple division of the beat, which is how I have notated it; but it can also be done with more swing—in other words, with a triplet feel.

DOUBLE FAKE WING TIME STEP

In all the following Fake Wings, as you land from the flap you begin the wing with the opposite foot.[7]

R	L		R	R		L	LR	R	R	L
							3-	s-	w	
dr	hop		fl-	ap		fl-	ap			dig
a	1	(&)	a	2	(&)	a	3	&	a	4

HALF FAKE WING TIME STEP BREAK

(Done after three one-bar Time Steps)

L	R	L	L	R	R	R	L	L	R	L
				3	-s-	w				
dr	hop		fl-	ap			dig	dr	hop	dig
a	1	(&)	a	2	&	a	3	&	a	4

This can be done as a more simplified Half Break just by stepping or flapping with the right foot in place of the Fake Wing.

Single Syncopated Fake Wing Time Step Break
(Done after two or six Time Steps)

R	L		R			L	LR	R	R		
							3	-s	– w		
dr	hop		st			fl-	ap				
a	1	(&)	a	(2)	(&)	a	3	&	a	(4)	(&)
			>							>	

L	LR	R	R		L	LR	R	R	L
	3	-s	- w			3-	s	- w	
fl-	ap				fl-	ap			dig
a	1	&	a	(2)	a	3	&	a	4
		>						>	

Double Five-Sound Wing Time Step [8]

							both feet tog
R	L		R	R	L	L	R
dr	hop		fl-	ap	fl-	ap	st
a	1	(&)	a	2	(&)	a	3	(&)	a	(4)

R	L		R	R	L	L		R	
dr	hop		fl-	ap	fl-	ap		st	
a	1	(&)	a	2	(&)	a	3	(&)	a	(4)
								>	

BO.LRLR		L	L		R	R		R	L
5-s-w		fl-	ap		sh-	fl	st	hl	dig
----1	(&)	a	2	(&)	a	3	&	a	4
								>	

In order to make a more challenging variation, on the last two counts substitute the ending of a Cramp Roll Time Step or a Fake Wing Time Step. These two variations will not alternate sides, however.

Five-Sound Wing Break

(Done after three two-bar Time Steps)

		front			ba				
L	R	L	L		R	L		L	R
dr	hop	fl-	ap		st	dig		dr	hop
a	1	(&)	a	2	(&)	a	3	(&)	a	4

		feet tog						
L	L	R		BO.LRLR	L	R	L
fl-	ap	st		5-s-w	hl	hl	dig
a	1	(&)	a	(2)	----3	&	a	4
		>					>

Examples of Anita's Time Steps

This list could go on forever. Hopefully, your list of original Time Steps will also start growing, beginning today.

Chug Time Step

						back			
R	L		R	L			R	R	L	R
ch	ch		ch	ch			dg	dr	hl	db-
a	4	(&)	a	1	(2)	(&)	a	3	&	a
>	>		>	>

R	R	R	R	R	R	L	L	R	L	R
db-	-le-	sh-	fl	st	hl	dg	dr	hl	Tip*	hl
a	4	&	a	1	&	a	2	&	a	3
			>			>			>

Alternates sides.

* **When you finish the Tip, keep the toe on the floor—to slide into the next Time Step or the Break on the left side.**

CHUG BREAK
(Done after one or three Time Steps)

a	(4)	(&)	a	(1)	(&)	a	2	(&)	a	(3)
L			L			R	R		L	
ch			ch			fl-	ap		ch*	
>			>						>	

a	4	(&)	a	(1)	(&)	a	2	&	a	3
R	R		L			R	R	L	L	R
fl-	ap		ch*			db-	le	-fl-	ap	hl†
			>							>

* On the flap chug, bring your weight up on the flap, and then recover down on the chug.

† On the double-flap heel, bring your weight up on the first flap. Keep it up on the second flap. End by bringing the weight down into a plie on the heel. Bring the second flap out to the side. Don't put your full weight on it.

Variation on Chug Time Step Break

a	(4)	(&)	a	(1)	(&)	a	2	(&)	a	(3)
L			L			R	R		L	
ch			ch			fl-	ap		ch	
>			>						>	

a	4	(&)	a	(1)	(&)	a	2	e	&	a	3
R	R		L			R	R	L	L	L	R
fl-	ap		ch			db-	le-	fl-	ap	hl	hl
			>						>		>

Extended Time Step in Duple Time
(Eight bars)

circle	R	cross	ba	uncross			forward....................................							
R	L	R	R	L	L	L	R		L		R		L	
sc	hop	br	st	sh-	fl	st	st		st		st		st	
1	2	&	3	&	4	&	(1)	&	(2)	&	(3)	&	(4)	&
>			>				>		>		>			

R		L	R	R	R	L	R		L	L	L	R
STO		STO	sh-	fl	ba-	ch	STO		sh-	fl	ba-	ch
1	(2)	3	&	4	&	1	&	(2)	&	3	&	4
>		>				>						
		>				>						

to left.........		in back of L........				to left...........		in back of L.................						
L	L		R	R	R		L	L		R	R	R		L
st	hl		br	st	hl		st	hl		br	st	hl		STO
1	&	(2)	&	3	&	(4)	&	1	(&)	2	&	3	(&)	4
														>

		circle R		ba of L / circle L							ba of R		
		R	L	R	R	L	R	L	L		R	R	R
freeze....		sc	hop	br	st	sc	hop	br	st		sh-	fl	st
(1)	(2)	3	4	&	1	&	(2)	&	3	&	4	&	a*
		>			>								

* **Be sure to notice that count 4 is a triplet.**

Clapping Variation

On the fifth and sixth bars, add clapping accents to counts 2 and 4 and &
after 1. The resulting step is:

to left............		in back of L.........			to left............			in back of L.................					
L	L	BO	R	R	R	BO	L	L	BO	R	R	R	L
st	hl	cla	br	st	hl	cla	st	hl	cla	br	st	hl	STO
1	&	2	&	3	&	4	&	1	&	2	&	3	(&) 4
	>				>			>					>

Bumbishay Time Step in a Measure of Five

	L	L	R	R	L
Bumbishay:	fl-	ap	ba	DIG*	st

* Put the ball of the foot down. Slide the foot forward into a dig, ending with the weight on the right heel, with the right toe lifted; the right leg and foot rotate out.

The Bumbishay travels slightly to the left. Lift the weight during the flap. Leave it up during the "ball DIG." Then bring it down on the final step. The more lift and more rotation, the fancier the step will look.

						front		ba		
R		R	L	R	R	L	L	R	L	L
dg		dr	hop	fl-	ap	fl-	ap	st	dg	dr
1	(&)	a	2	(&)	a	3	(&) a	4	(&) a	5	(&) a
>									>	

					front		ba		
R		L	L	R	R	L	R	L	R	R	L
hop		Bumbishay.................					dr	hop	fl-	ap	st
1	(&) a	2	& a	3	(&) a	4	(&) a	5	(&) a
>		>		>					>

Does not alternate sides.

Bumbishay Break in Fives

(Done after two or six Bumbishay Time Steps)

	1	(&)	a	2	(&)	a	3	(&)	a	4	(&)	a	5	(&)	a
									front			ba			
	R		R	L		R	R		L	L		R	L		L
	dig		dr	hop		fl-	ap		fl-	ap		st	dig		dr
	>												>		

	1	(&)	a	2	(&)	a	3	(&)	a	4	(&)	a	5
						front			ba				
	R		L	L		R	R		L	R		R	L
	hop		fl-	ap		fl-	ap		st	dg		dr	hop
	>								>			>	

	1	(&)	a	2	&	a	3	(&)	a	4	&	a	5	(&)	a
	L	R	R	L	L	R	L	L	R	R	L	R			
	hop	Bumbishay............					Bumbishay*............					Bumbishay*...			
	>						>			>					

	1	&	a	2	(&)	a	3	&	a	4	(&)	a	5	(&)	a
												back			
	R	L	L	R	L	L	R	R	L	R	L	R			
	....				Bumbishay*............					dr	hop	st			
				>				>							

Alternates sides.

* **Start those Bumbishays with a draw step instead of a flap.**

Time Step Play

1. Mix and match any of the Time Steps and Breaks that work to-gether. For instance, dance six Triple-Triple Cramp Roll Time Steps followed by one Traditional Triple-Triple Time Step Break.

2. Whenever possible, try the duple Time Steps with a triplet feel, and the triplet Time Steps as duples. It will help if you use corresponding music.

3. Dance the Time Steps three different ways when possible—with stomps, with digs, and with shuffles (refer to the first Buggy Ride Time Step as an example).

4. Take away and add sounds to the above Time Steps, thereby creating many exciting variations.

5. Choreograph and improvise your own Breaks for the above Time Steps.

6. Create your own one-bar, two-bar, and four-bar Time Steps. Create or improvise the appropriate breaks for them.

7. Create Time Steps in the measures of your choice (i.e., 6s, 7s, 11s, etc.).

8. Choreograph a whole dance that uses many of these Time Steps with additional transitional steps of your own. Use music, and be sensitive to its phrasing. In this chapter, I have assumed that the phrases last eight or sixteen bars, but in many styles of music the phrases last twelve bars, such as the boogie woogie and the blues, so it is important to listen to the entire piece of music before starting to choreograph.

8

Traditional Tap: Flash

TAP DANCERS IN THE 1920s, striving to be the most original and most dazzling, began to invent steps that moved the entire body and ventured into the air. These dancers created a whole new category of steps called "flash steps," which, for two reasons, were often used as the grand finale of an act. First, the music was often quite loud at the end of a song, and flash steps didn't have to be heard to be appreciated; second, and probably even more important, the audiences went (and still go) wild when dancers perform flash steps.

Two flash steps, called "Over-the-Top" and "Pulling the Trenches," are attributed to Toots Davis, who became famous for them while dancing in the "Darktown Follies," an innovative and successful musical comedy that opened in Harlem in 1913.[1] The other important flash step is the "Wing" which combines air movement with tap rhythms. The great tapper Baby Lawrence attributed the first Wing to Jack Wiggins. As Lawrence explained, "People started to say he looked like he had wings,"and the name was born.[2] A great variety of Wings started to emerge in the 1930s, with the most amazing of them all being the Five-Tap Wing, originated by Frank Condos. Condos had what was called a "flash act" with Mattie King, called "King and King." Condos' act ended with a challenge dance that, in his words, "piled on the wings," to the audience's delight.[3]

Flash steps continue to impress audiences; today, however, they are also used in rhythmical phrases, rather than just repetitively for applause.

The intended mystery of flash steps is the total ease with which they are done. Without actually going up or down, flash dancers seem to be weightless as they skim along the floor. They don't defy gravity with balletic leaps or plunge into the ground with modern dance falls. Rather, they must have a perfect balance between lifting up and being grounded. If they lift too high, they miss all the sounds; if they don't lift enough, the step is labored. Subtle balance is the secret to all flash steps.

In this chapter, I describe each flash step and the most efficient way to accomplish it. I also give suggestions to promote progressive acquisition of each thrilling trick, beginning with preparation exercises and proceeding to increasingly difficult drills. At the end of the chapter, I give examples of combinations that integrate a variety of flash steps into fascinating rhythms.

Note: For each flash step, after you have perfected the preparation exercise, practice the flash step while sitting to assure yourself of the coordination and correct action of the legs. THIS IS VERY IMPORTANT. Most of the flash steps require unusual changes of weight or sickled (rolled in) feet. Trying flash steps without accomplishing the necessary prerequisites could result in injury if you are not clear where your weight should be.

When you have practiced the flash step while sitting, try the step holding firmly to a stable support. Either grip a ballet barre, or stand in between two sturdy chairs, holding on to their backs. Use the strength in your arms to help suspend yourself. As the flash step becomes easier, begin to release your hold on the support little by little. When you find that you're getting close to accomplishing the flash step with your hands only resting on the bar or chairs, you are ready to work on the drills without support.

Over The Top

In an Over-the-Top, you literally hop forward over your own leg as it slides backward.

Preparation

1. Step on the left foot in back of the right foot.
2. Slide the right foot back next to the left, keeping all your weight on the left foot. Sickle the right foot so that the sliding sound is made with the outside rim of the shoe. It is extremely important that you have no weight on the right foot.
3. As you are sliding the right foot, hop onto the left foot while traveling forward. Don't hop too high. You are traveling forward while your sliding foot is traveling backward.
4. Hold.

Reverse.

As you increase in expertise, the takeoff of the hop occurs exactly at the same time as the leg slides backward, still without putting any weight on the sliding leg. Bend over from the waist and feel the slight lift from the pelvis. Swing your arms in opposition to your legs. This will help you get the feeling of an Over-the-Top, although you aren't yet really doing one.

Preparation for an Over-the-Top.

Hopping over the sliding leg.

Landing from an Over-the-Top.

Drill I

Do the above exercise, but now execute a true Over-the-Top by sliding the right foot under the left hopping foot. The sliding sound will continue to come from the outside rim of the right shoe. The more plie you have as you hop over your leg—and, therefore, the more bent the right knee is—the more of your leg you can hop over and the fancier the step appears. Try it, and you'll understand what I mean. As is true of the preparation, you should be bent over from the waist, lifting in the pelvis, swinging arms in opposition to the legs, not actually putting any weight on the sliding foot. Find the balance of up and down. If you're too high, the magical illusion will not exist. If you're not high enough, the step will be labored or you will hurt yourself by putting weight on the sliding leg.

Drill II

L back	hop fr L*	L	R in ba
st	slide ba R*	land	Tip
1	2	3	4

L	R back	L	R
hop	st	Over-the-Top	land
1	2	3	4

Does not alternate sides.

* From now on, I will notate this part of the step as Over-the-Top on the right side (since you are making the sliding sound with your right foot).

Drill III

L back	R	L back	R
Tip	hop	st	Over-the-Top
1	2	3	4

L	R back	L	R
land	st	Over-the-Top	land
1	2	3	4

Does not alternate sides.

DRILL IV

Do Drill II, followed immediately by Drill III. This does not alternate sides.

Over-the-Top Play
Discover a way to accomplish an Over-the-Top by reversing the direction of the sliding leg so that it slides from back to front. Incorporate this new Over-the-Top into a combination.

Pulling the Trenches

Pulling the Trenches (or Trenches, for short) gives the illusion of running on ice without getting anywhere.

Try the Trenches, sitting down first. Since the movement of the arms is so important, I suggest that you practice Trenches without holding on to anything. Be cautious in the beginning by being sure that no weight is on the sliding leg.

DRILL I

Start with your weight on the left leg, with a bent knee; extend the right leg out to the side in a parallel position.

1   Swing the right leg to the left, into a bent position—with the right knee lifted and the right foot in back of the left. At the same time, swing both arms to the left in front of you.[4]

&   This swing of the leg and arms will give you the lift and the momentum for the left foot to slide out to the side. When you first try this, feel the whole ball of the foot sliding on the floor for a moment. THERE SHOULD BE NO WEIGHT ON THAT SLIDING LEG. As you become more advanced, extend the slide as long as possible and sickle the sliding foot so the outside rim of the shoe slides on the floor. It is similar to the beginning of a Fake Wing, except that it is a much larger movement.[5]

2   Land on the right foot, with the left leg extended out to the side, off the floor.

Repeat on the other side. Continue to alternate right and left.

Just as you do for an Over-the-Top, you should now be bent over from the waist. This is both for the look of the step and to help with the necessary lift. When you have mastered this drill, start to slide the leg diagonally back instead of to the side. The leg should continue to slide on the outside of a sickled foot. THIS IS VERY IMPORTANT. I cannot stress enough that you should not actually put any weight on that sickled sliding foot.

Pullbacks

A Pullback is a quick air flap. It is performed with two feet at the same time, with two feet that sound one at a time, with one foot that lands on the same foot, or with one foot that lands on the opposite foot. The easiest way to do a Pullback is in a backward direction.

Most students I know can do Pullbacks from a flat-footed position, rolling the weight slightly back into the heels and making that first brush sound on the way into the air. Many teachers believe that it is best to teach a Pullback from this flat-footed position because it is so much easier to do and does not frustrate the students. The problem is, this is really not a Pullback since there is no illusion of weightlessness. Learning it this way will not help you do it correctly. It is also impossible to incorporate the Pullback in a variety of combinations, since you must always be in a flat-footed preparatory position.

The best tap dancers can execute a Pullback cleanly and easily, starting on the balls of the feet with their heels very slightly off the floor. This requires that you jump just the right distance off the floor, then make the brush sound of the flap on the way down. It may be more difficult in the beginning; but, once you learn it, it will become more and more effortless. You will have total control over the sound and rhythm, and you will be able to incorporate your Pullbacks easily and quickly into any combination.

Preparation

1   Stand on the left leg. Lift the right foot slightly off the floor by lifting the knee and flexing the foot very slightly.

(e)

(&)

a 2   With the right foot, do a very crisp, quick, tiny flap backward.

Repeat at least eight times, then change sides. Strive for speed and crispness of sound. This step is not done with a totally relaxed ankle. Use the entire leg, but also flex the foot slightly at the beginning of each pullback. This combined use of leg and foot will ultimately give you control over the sound and rhythm of your Pullbacks.

Pullbacks are especially easy to learn from a sitting position. Practice all the following drills sitting down first.

Single Pullback—Both Feet at the Same Time

DRILL I

jump	jump	jump				(up) pull- back
1	2	3	(e)	(&)	a	4

The jumps are all done on the balls of the feet, with the heels lifted only slightly off the floor. The Pullback should have the same easy lift as the jumps. The sound of the Pullbacks should happen *on the way down from the jump*. Many students bend backward at the waist when trying the Pullback. For the health of your back, and for better balance, be sure that your weight remains over your feet the entire time. The Pullbacks will move you slightly backward, but the better you get at them, the less you will travel.

DRILL II

Gradually decrease the number of jumps and increase the number of Pullbacks (for example, first try jump, jump, Pullback, Pullback) until you can do Pullbacks all in a row. Keep checking that you are making the sound on the way down. Make interesting patterns of jumps and Pullbacks that last two bars (for instance, jump, Pullback, jump, Pullback, Pullback, jump, jump, Pullback).

Double Pullback—Four Sounds

A Double Pullback is executed with two feet and is done as follows:

	R	L	R	L
jump up	br back	br back	land	land

Begin by jumping slightly up with both feet at the same time, as you would for a Single Pullback. On your way down, do the Double Pullback. The resulting sound should be an even four-sound roll. Follow the same procedure for learning as you did for the single pullback.

Drills I and II

Practice Drills I and II of Single Pullbacks, substituting the Double Pullbacks for the Single Pullbacks. Practice the drills on both sides.

Drill III

Learn to do a Double Pullback from an open position of the legs to a closed position.

Do Drill I. Gradually open the legs on the three jumps. Bring them back together as you execute the Double Pullback. The brushes should go in toward the center instead of backward. This drill will also serve as a good preparation for learning a Wing.

Drill IV

fr	tog				fr	tog		
R	L	R L R L			R	L	R L R L	
st	st	db-le-pb			st	st	db-le-pb	
a	1	(&)	a. . .2	(&)	a	3	(&)	a. . .4

open					close			
R R L L		R	L		R L R L	R	L	R
db-le-fl-ap*		hl	hl		†db-le-pb	hl	hl	hl
a . . 1	(&)	a	2	(&)	a . . 3	&	a	4

* A double flap produces the same four sounds as a Double Pullback. Plie as a preparation. Throw two flaps out, right and then left, without pause in between, while opening your legs. End perched on the balls of your feet, with straight legs.

† Even though the preparation to the first three Pullbacks in this combination is two steps rather than a jump, you should be standing on the balls of your feet prior to the Pullbacks. Before the last Pullback of this combination, however, your feet will be flat on the floor. Execute the Pullback in exactly the same way, lifting the body slightly off the floor, and making the sounds on the way down. Don't be tempted, instead, to lift the toes as preparation.

One-Legged Pullbacks

There are two types of One-Legged Pullbacks: Pullbacks that hop up in the air and flap on the way down (pb or pullba), and those that go up in the air, brush on the way down with one foot, then land on the opposite foot (pb-ch). The following drills combine the two. As in most flash steps, begin by learning these drills sitting down, then supporting yourself with your hands on a barre or on two sturdy chairs.

DRILL I

1	2	(e)	(&)	a	3	4
R	R			R	R	R
hop	hop			pullba		hop

1	(e)	(&)	a	2	3	e	&	a	4
R				R	R	L	L	R	L
hop				pullba	hop	sh-	fl	pb-	ch

DRILL II

R	L	L	L	R	R	R	L	L	L	R	R
st	sh-	fl	st	sh-	fl	st	sh-	fl	st	sh-	fl
1	&	a	2	&	a	3	&	a	4	&	a

R	L	L	R	L	L	R	L	L	R	L	L
st	sh-	fl	hop	sh-	fl	hop	sh-	fl	hop	sh-	fl
1	&	a	2	&	a	3	&	a	4	&	a

R	L	L	R	L	R	R	L	R	L	L	R	L	R	R	L
hp	sh-	fl	pb-	ch	sh-	fl	pb-	ch	sh-	fl	pb-	ch	sh-	fl	pb-
1	e	&	a	2	e	&	a	3	e	&	a	4	e	&	a

R	L	L	R	R	L	L	R	R	L	L	R	R	L	L	R	L
ch	sh-	fl	pull	ba	sh-	fl	pull	ba	sh-	fl	pull	ba	sh-	fl	pb-	(ch)
1	e	&	a	2	e	&	a	3	e	&	a	4	e	&	a	1

Reverses sides.

DRILL III: ONE-LEGGED PULLBACKS FROM A FLATFOOT

R		L	L	R	L	L	R	R	L	R	R
STO		sh-	fl	pb-	ch	hl	sh-	fl	pb-	ch	hl
1	(&)	a	2	&	a	3	&	a	4	&	a

>

Alternates sides. Repeat three times: right side, left side, and right side. Then:

L	L	R	L	L	R	R	L	L	L	R	R
sh-	fl	pb-	ch	hl	sh-	fl	pullba		hl	st	hl
1	&	a	2	&	a	3	&	a	4	&	a

The entire combination reverses sides.

DRILL IV

Perform the Maxi Ford exercise described in Chapter 3.

Pullback Play

Try any of the above exercises, pullbacking in any possible direction—side, diagonal, front, opening, closing, crossing, and so on. Use the same technique no matter what direction you do your Pullbacks. Be sure to lift up prior to the Pullback and to make the sound on the way down.

Wings

Preparation

There are two methods for performing Wings.

FIRST METHOD

1 Start in a plie on the left foot, with the right foot turned out very slightly, heel lifted and resting on the floor next to the left foot. Slide the right foot diagonally forward and to the right, making a sliding sound with the whole right ball, leading with the toe until it comes just off the floor. At the same time, lift your weight out of the plie until the left leg straightens.

(&)

a 2 Flap back on a diagonal, into the original position. At the same time, plie.

Repeat this exercise a minimum of eight times, gradually increasing speed. Then change sides.

SECOND METHOD

1 Start in a plie on the left foot, with right foot turned parallel, heel lifted, resting on the floor next to the left foot. Sickle the right foot until it is resting on the outside rim of the shoe. Slide the outside of the shoe out to the side, flicking it until it comes off the floor slightly. The sliding sound is made with the outside of the toe tap. At the same time, lift to a straight left leg. Once the right foot is off the floor, the foot should not be sickled or pronated.

(&) a

2 Flap directly sideward in toward the standing foot, into the beginning position. At the same time, plie.

The second method is more difficult and more dangerous, because of the sickled foot. It is also more impressive, since it gives a greater illusion of weightlessness and rubber-leggedness. Before doing the drills, choose the method you are going to try.

Two-Legged Three-Sound Wing

The first sound is the slide out. The next two sounds are made by the flap coming in with both feet at the same time.

DRILL I

			3 –	s –	w
jump	jump	jump	slide	fl –	ap
1	2	3	&	a	4

DRILL II

Gradually decrease the number of jumps while increasing the number of wings. For instance, first try jump, jump, Wing, Wing. Try variations until you can do four Wings in a row. Then make interesting patterns of jumps and Wings that last two bars (for instance: jump, Wing, Wing, jump, jump, Wing, Wing, Wing).

Five-Sound Wing

The first sound is of two feet sliding out at the same time. Then do a Double Pullback on the way in: right foot brushing in, left foot brushing in, right foot landing, left foot landing. Or you can do the reverse.

DRILLS I AND II

Do Drills I and II from the section on Three-Sound Wings, substituting Five-Sound Wings for the Three-Sound Wings.

DRILL III

R	L	BO.	RLRL		
st	st	5 –	s –	w	(lift right foot off floor immediately on count 2)
a	1	&	a.. 2	(3)	(4)

Repeat three times on the same side. Then:

R	L	BO.	RLRL		
st	st	5 –	s –	w	(ending with ball-tap)
a	1	&	a.. 2	(3)	(4)

Do only one time. In order to change sides, the last sound with the left foot will be a ball-tap instead of a step. Lift the left foot to begin the other side. Reverses sides.

DRILL IV

R	L	BO.	RLRL		R	L	BO.	RLRL	BO.
st	st	5 –	s – w		st	st	5 –	s – w	5 –
a	1	&	a . . 2	(&)	a	3	&	a . . 4	&

RLRL			BO.	RLRL		R	L
s – w			5 – s – w			hl	Tip
a . . 1	(&)	(a)	(2) &	a . . 3	(&)	a	4

Reverses sides.

One-Legged Three-Sound Wing

As is true of the one-legged Pullback, there are two types of one-legged Wings—those that land on the Winging foot and those that land on the opposite foot. A Right Wing that does not change sides starts with the weight on the right foot—wings out to the side and flaps in with the right foot. A Right Wing that does change sides starts with the weight on the right foot, wings out with the right foot, brushes in with the right foot, and lands on the left foot. You will know which one I'm talking about by looking carefully at which feet are making the sounds.

DRILL I

fr	ba					back	tog
R	L	R	R	R	R	L	R
st	Tip*	3	- s -	w	hl	st	st
a	1	e	&	a	2	3	4

* After the Tip, as you do the Wing, lift the left knee up, similar to a retire in ballet.

Reverses sides.

Drill II

1	&	2	e	&	a	3	(4)
fr	kick	side diag			cr	fr	of R
R	L	R	R	R	L	L	
st	br	3	-	s	- w	br st	
1	&	2	e	&	a	3	(4)

1	&	2	e	&	a	3	(4)
ba	kick	side diag			cr	ba	of R
R	L	R	R	R	L	L	
st	br	3	-	s	- w	br st	
1	&	2	e	&	a	3	(4)

1	&	2	e	&	a	3	(4)
fr	kick	side diag			cr	fr	of R
R	L	R	R	R	L	L	
st	br	3	-	s	- w	br st	
1	&	2	e	&	a	3	(4)

a	1	e	&	a	2	&	(3)	&	(4)	&
ba	kick				back	back		side		fr
R	L	R	R	L	R	R		L		R
st	br	3	-	s - w	Tip	st		st		st
a	1	e	&	a	2	&	(3)	&	(4)	&

Reverses sides.

The Pendulum Wing.

Pendulum Wing

Pendulum Wings are repetitive One-Legged Wings in which the nonwinging leg brushes with a kick front, then back, then front, then back, and so on. Kick the leg high; it will look more impressive and will help you achieve the necessary lift.

DRILL I

fr				ba				fr				*cr fr of R		
L	R	R	R	L	R	R	R	L	R	R	R	L		L
br	3 -	s -	w	br	3 -	s -	w	br	3 -	s -	w	br		st
1	e	&	a	2	e	&	a	3	e	&	a	4	(e)	&

Alternates sides.

*** The left brush step crosses in front of the right foot. To repeat on the other side, circle the right leg back and around to right before brushing right to the front.**

DRILL II

On count 4 of Drill I, do:

cr fr of R			
L	L	L	
br	st	hl	
4	e	&	(a)

DRILL III

On count 4 of Drill I, do:

cr fr of R			
L	L	R	L
br	st	dr	hl
4	e	&	a

This is a more difficult variation because there is no break in the rhythm or time to prepare for the other side.

Drill IV

fr				ba				fr		ba				
L	R	R	R	L	R	R	R	L		L	R	R	R	L
br	3	-	s	-	w	br	3	-	s	-	w	br		

fr				ba				fr		ba				
L	R	R	R	L	R	R	R	L		L	R	R	R	L
br	3	-	s	-	w	br	3	-	s	-	w	br	br	3	-	s	-	w	st
1	e	&	a	2	e	&	a	3	(e)	&	a	4	e	&

ba				fr		ba				fr				
R	L	L	L	R		R	L	L	L	R	L	L	L	R
br	3	-	s	-	w	br		br	3	-	s	-	w	br	3	-	s	-	w	st
1	e	&	a	2	(e)	&	a	3	e	&	a	4	e	&

This combination does not reverse. After four repetitions, stop, catch your breath, and do the other side.

Scissor Wings

Scissor Wings are One-Legged Wings in which the nonwinging leg Toe-Tips are alternating front and back. As you wing, you should lift the toe-tipping knee as high as possible.

Drill I

ba				fr				ba				fr		ba
L	R	R	R	L	R	R	R	L	R	R	R	L		R
Tip	3	-	s	-	w	Tip	3	-	s	-	w	Tip	3	-	s	-	w	st		Tip
1	e	&	a	2	e	&	a	3	e	&	a	4	(e)	&

Reverses sides.

Drill II

Same as Drill I; but on count 4, add:

fr		back		
L		R	R	L
st		sh	-	fl	hop
4		e	&	a

Fake Wings

For lack of a better name, I call the wings in which you don't really lift your weight totally off the floor, "Fake Wings." I now describe three kinds of Fake Wings in the following three drills.

DRILL I. NONCHANGING FAKE WING

To start, stand on the right foot.

1   wing the right foot out, lifting your weight up; at the same time, land on the ball of the left foot with a straight leg

&   br R in toward L

a   step R

2   dig L

Does not alternate sides.

DRILL II. CHANGEOVER FAKE WING

Start by standing on the right foot.

1   wing R foot out, lifting your weight up; at the same time, land on the ball of the L foot with a straight leg

&   br R back

a   hl-drop L

2   Toe-Tip R in back

(3)

(4)

Alternates sides.

DRILL III. TOE-TIP FAKE WING

This drill requires strong arches!

Stand on the right foot to start.

1   Toe-Tip L foot in back of R. Lift weight up, straightening L leg; for a second, put weight on L Toe-Tip. Because your weight is on the Toe-Tip for so short a time, and because your body is lifted up, there should be no strain. Lift arms at the same time

   e   wing R foot out. L Toe-Tip is still supporting you

   &   brush R foot in

   a   land on R foot

   2   step L next to R

(3)

(4)

Alternates sides.

Wing Play

Experiment with a more difficult Wing: slide the feet out, do a shuffle while your weight is in the air, and land with feet close together—for a total of four sounds.

Now try that famous Five-Tap Wing: slide the feet out, shuffle while your weight is in the air and flap with the feet coming together to finish. If you accomplish this one, you are ready for the "Big Time."

Rhythmic Combinations That Include Flash Steps

As I have mentioned, the traditional way of using flash steps is to do as many as possible, one right after another, as fast as possible. Feel free to do that for yourself, drilling all different combinations of the above flash steps.

In the remainder of this chapter, I give examples of combinations that incorporate the various flash steps in rhythmically interesting ways. Some of them are show-stopping combinations; some are more subtle.

PHRASE I. THREE-SOUND WING COMBINATION

BOTH		R		L	R	R	L	R	R	L	R	L		L
3 - s - w		hl		hl	dig	dr	hl	br	st	dr	hl	STA		STO
4	&	1		2		3	&	4	&	1	&	2	&	3	(&)	4
				>				>				>		>

R	L	R	L		R		L	R	L	R		L		R	L	R	L
4 -	s-	cr-	roll*		STO		4-	s-	cr-	roll*		STO		4 -	s -	cr-	roll*
1	&	a	2		3		4	&	a	1		2		3	&	4	&
					>							>					

in to L ft	in to R ft

R	L	L	L	R		R		L	R	R	R	L	L	L
br	3 -	s -	w	br		st		br	3 -	s -	w	br	st	hl
1	&	2	&	3		4		1	&	2	&	3	&	4

cr fr L   turning counter-clockwise†

R	L	L	L	R	R	R	L	R	L	R		L
br	3 -	s -	w	br**	st	hl	hl	td	td	st		st
1	&	2	&	3	&	4	&	1	&	2		3

Reverses sides.

* To do a cramp roll, jump off the floor, and land on the first ball of foot, second ball, heel-drop, and the other heel-drop, ending with the weight flat on both feet.

† Turn counterclockwise as you do the brush step heel heel toe-drop toe-drop, finishing the turn on the first step on count 2. The majority of the turn occurs on the toe-drops by pivoting on the heels. Cross as much as possible on the brush step heel to get off to a good start on the turn.

PHRASE II. SCISSOR WING COMBINATION (WITH ONE CHANGEOVER WING)

Begin the combination by stepping on the right foot on count 8.

			Changeover	

L	R	R	R	L		L	R	R	R	L		L	R	R	L
Tip	3 -	s -	w	Tip		Tip	3 -	s -	w	Tip		Tip	3 -	s -	w
1	&	2	&	3		4	&	1	&	2		3	&	4	&
>				>		>				>		>			

R		R	R	L	R	R		L		L		L	L	L	LA
Tip		5-s-riff*..................						Tip		Tip		4-s-riff*..............			
1		2	&	3	&	4		1		2		3	&	4	&
>								>		>					

Reverses sides.

First, do all Tips in the back. For a more advanced step, alternate the Tips back and front in your own way.

* For instructions on a five-sound-riff and four-sound-riff, see Chapter 6, "Fastest Feet," under the heading, "Riffs."

PHRASE III. PENDULUM WING COMBINATION

Begin combination by stepping right on count 8.

fr				ba				br				cr fr of R			
L	R	R	R	L	R	R	R	L	R	R	R	L	L	R	L
br	3	- s -	w	br	3	- s -	w	br	3	- s -	w	br	st	dr	hl
1	e	&	a	2	e	&	a	3	e	&	a	4	e	&	a*

travel to ba R diag........................				to L		travel to ba R diag..........									
R	L	R	L	R	L	R	R	L	L	R	L	R	L	R	L
st	dr	hl	st	dr	hl	st	hl	st	hl	st	dr	hl	st	dr	hl
1	e	&	a	2	e	&	a	3	e	&	a	4	e	&	a
>		>			>	>		>		>			>		

fr				ba				fr				cr fr of L			
R	L	L	L	R	L	L	L	R	L	L	L	R	R	L	R
br	3	- s -	w	br	3	- s -	w	br	3	- s -	w	br	st	dr	hl
1	e	&	a	2	e	&	a	3	e	&	a	4	e	&	a*

		both feet on floor													
L		R		R		L	R	R	L	R	R	L	L		
st		st		hl		hl	dg	dr	hl	fl-	ap	st	hl†		
1	(e)	(&)	a	(2)	(e)	&	(a)	3	e	&	a	4	e	&	a

Alternates sides.

* Notice that the first and third measures are Drill III, under "Pendulum Wings."

† Do the fl-ap st hl like a cramp roll, lifting the weight up on the flap, and ending by bringing the weight down into a plie on the step heel. Ending with your weight down into a plie will also prepare you to start again with the wings on the other side.

PHRASE IV. CHANGEOVER PULLBACK COMBINATION

This is a traditional show-stopping combination that is also a lot of fun to do.

fr	back		fr	back			fr	back			fr	back	
R	L	L	R	L	R	R	L	R	L	L	R	L	R	R	L
ST	sh-	fl	pb-	CH	sh-	fl	pb-	CH	sh-	fl	pb-	CH	sh-	fl	pb-
1	e	&	a	2	e	&	a	3	e	&	a	4	e	&	a
>				>				>				>			

fr	back		ba	front		fr	back		ba	front		fr	back		
R	L	L	R	L	L	R	L	L	R	L	L	R	L	L	R	(L)
CH	sh-	fl	hop	sh-	fl	*HOP	sh-	fl	hop	sh-	fl	*HOP	sh-	fl	pb-(CH)
1	e	&	a	2	e	&	a	3	e	&	a	4	e	&	a	(1)
>				>				>				>			

Changes sides.

* This HOP is almost like a chug that comes slightly off the floor and lands on the whole foot. Anything CAPITALIZED in this combination lands on the whole foot. During the last two bars, the legs are like scissors: after the right foot CHUGS forward, the left foot shuffles in back; after the right foot hops backward, the left foot shuffles in front.

PHRASE V. FAKE WING COMBINATION WITH AN OVER THE TOP

		side wing		in to R				
R	R	L		L	L	R	R	
fl-	ap	slide*		fl-	ap	fl-	ap	
a	1	(&)	a	(2)	(&)	a	3	(&)	a	4	(&)
		>						

side wing		in to R				side wing	
L		L		R		L	
slide*		fl-	ap	fl-	ap	slide*	
a	(1)	(&)	a	2	(&)	a	3	(&)	a	(4)	(&)
>						>	

* This is the sliding part of the Wing only. You are standing on the R leg as you make the sliding sound. Make the sound an accent by extending it a little longer than usual within the count.

						Wing R†				forward	
L	L		R	R		L	L	R	L	R	R
fl-	ap		fl-	ap		fl-	ap†	br	hl	br	st
a	1	(&)	a	2	(&)	a	3	&	a	4	&

		Wing R†				forward					
R	L	L	R	L	R	R	R		L	L	
hl	fl-	ap†	br	hl	br	st	hl		fl-	ap	
a	1	&	a	2	&	a	3	(&)	a	4	(&)

† This is a Fake Wing. When you land on the flap, wing the R foot out at the same time.

			side wing			in to R					
R	R		L			L	L		R		
fl-	ap		slide*			fl-	ap		st		
a	1	(&)	a	(2)	(&)	a	3	(&)	a	(4)	(&)
			>						>		

	ba			ba			ba						
L	R	R	R	L	R	R	R	L	R	R	L		
TIP	3-	s-	w	TIP	3-	s-	w	st	dr	ba-	ch		
(a)	1	e	&	a	2	e	&	a	3	&	a	4	(&)

			back			side	front		‡back		
R	R		L			L	R		R		
br	st		Tip			leap	Tip		leap		
a	1	(&)	a	(2)	(&)	a	3	(&)	(a)	4	(&)
			>				>				

				ba			side				
L		R	L	R	L	L	L	R	R		
Over-the-Top		land	Tip	hp	sh-fl	st	fl-	ap			
a	(1)	(&)	a	2	(&)	a	. 3	&	a	4	(&)
>			>								

‡ For the fanciest look, bring the right leg out and around the left before leaping in back of the left.

Reverses sides.

PHRASE VI. OVER-THE-TOP COMBINATION WITH TIME STEP

back			back
L	R	L	R
st	Over-the-Top	land	Tip
1	2	3	4

	back		
L	R	L	R
hop	st	Over-the-Top	land
1	2	3	4

back			back	
L	L	R	L	R
sh -	fl	hop	st	Over-the-Top
1	(&)	a	2	3	4

	back		
L	R	L	R
land	st	Over-the-Top	land
1	2	3	4

back			back
L	R	L	R
st	Over-the-Top	land	Tip
1	2	3	4

		back			
L		R		L	R
hop		st		Over-the-Top	land
1		2		3	4

back							
L		R		L	R	L	
Tip		hop		st	fl-	ap	br
1		2		3	(&) a	4	(&) a

front	back				
L	R	L	L	R	L
st	st	sh-	-fl	hop	st
1	(&) a	2	(&) a	3	4
	>			>	

Reverses sides.

You might have noticed that this combination incorporates one of the Over the Top drills.

As a variation, you can substitute four Through the Trenches (L R L R) in the fifth and sixth measures on counts 1 3 1 3.

PHRASE VII. SHIM SHAM COMBINATION WITH OVER-THE-TOP
Refer to the fourth step of the Shim Sham Shimmy in Chapter 7.

PHRASE VIII. TURNING WALTZ CLOG COMBINATION WITH PULLBACK CHANGE

to R/ to side					to L/ to side				
R	L	L	L	R	L	R	R	R	L
STO	sh -	fl	ball-	change	STO	sh -	fl	ball-	change
1	&	2	&	3	(&) 1	&	2	&	3	(&)
>					>				

1st clockwise turn								Beg of 2nd turn					ba
R	L	L	R	L	R	L	R	R	L	L	L	R	
STO	sh-	fl	pb-	ch	br	hl	st	hl	br	st	hl	br	
1	(&)	a	2	&	a	3	&	1	&	2	&	3	&
>						>		>		>			

Does not alternate sides.

You can also do a series of turns by repeating consecutively the third and fourth measures only.

PHRASE IX. TURN WITH PULLBACK CHANGE, IN TRIPLETS

1st clockwise turn										Beg of 2nd turn	
R	L	L	R	L	R	L	R	R	R	L	L
hl	sh-	fl	pb-	ch	Tip	hl	br	st	hl	br	st
1	&	a	2	&	a	3	&	a	4	&	a
>						>		>			
>											

		Beg of 3rd turn									
L	R	R	R	L	L	R	L	R	L	R	R
hl	br	st	hl	sh -	fl	pb-	ch	Tip	hl	br	st
1	&	a	2	&	a	3	&	a	4	&	a
>			>						>		

Does not alternate sides. Repeat consecutively to do a series of turns.

PHRASE X. TURN WITH A FIVE-SOUND WING

cr fr		facing R	side		face ba	
R	L		L	R	R	BO
st*	br	(leap)	land	br	st†	5-
1	&	(2)	&	3	&	4

* Start by facing front with your weight on the left foot. As you cross the right foot in front of the left, face side.

† When you finish the brush step, you should be facing back, with the right foot crossed in back of the left.

turn to fr	beg of 2nd turn			back	back	front
L R L R	R	L	L	L	R	R	L
s - wing‡	hl	br	st	hl	br	ball-	change§
& . . 1	&	2	&	3	&	4	&

‡   As you five-sound wing, your feet end crossed in reverse with the right foot in front of the left, and at the same time, you turn a half turn clockwise to face front.

§   The brush back causes you to face back. During the ball change, you pivot to face front on the change.

You've tried and you've tried, and you still can't achieve a Pullback. Don't feel bad. It might take you a week to learn, or it might take years. When I was a child, my tap teacher gave anyone who accomplished a Pullback for the first time a silver dollar. She didn't have to part with very many of them.

Flash steps give you a greater range. I have seen some master hoofers, however, dance for hours, never do a Wing, and still leave me with my mouth open, astonished at the beauty, speed, and variety of their intricate footwork.

So keep working on those flash steps, but don't despair if they have not reached the finesse of your other dancing.

9

New Tap: Orchestrated Tap

AMONG RHYTHM TAP ENTHUSIASTS, chorus line dancing was viewed as simplistic and often less than artistic. Although there were exceptions, most chorus lines danced simple combinations with faked flash steps. The dancers put on a "show" with their movement without executing the actual sounds of the flash steps. The excitement of chorus line tap was the visual kaleidoscope effect of body parts moving in perfect unison (usually belonging to beautiful women), rather than the speed, subtlety, and sound of rhythm tap. Individuality and rhythm were subordinated to geometric design and glamour.

The kings of chorus line choreography in the early 1900s—such as Ned Wayburn, David Bennett, and Busby Berkeley—didn't even mention dance ability as a prerequisite to being chosen at an audition. Busby Berkeley, who epitomizes chorus-line dancing on film, regarded "the horde of gorgeous creatures who apply to him for jobs, and the comparative few who get jobs, the way a nut-and-bolt manufacturer regards his products. When Berkeley looks at a girl, he looks at her face and her figure. He looks at her arms and hands. . . . If they're all right, he looks at her legs. And they have to be good!"[1]

Today, in many dancing school recitals, in popular dance on television, and in some Broadway shows, chorus lines are still popular. But innovative modern rhythm tap choreographers are now developing new forms of ensemble tap dances that are polyphonic, rather than in strict unison.

Music is said to be polyphonic if it consists of two or more layered parts, each having individual melodic significance. Polyphony was developed in the 9th century.[2] Tap dance is starting to catch up, with choreographers creating exciting polyphonic ensemble dances that borrow from musical ensemble forms, and concentrate on the complex music of the feet. I will call this "Orchestrated Tap."

Orchestrated Tap is especially exciting because it can result in fascinating movement design through space, as well as impressive, complex percussion. It can utilize the individuality of the dancers within group forms. Orchestrated Tap is one of the most important developments of tap dance in recent years.

In this chapter, I describe five different types of orchestrations for tap dance. After describing each type, I give an example of combinations for two groups (or two dancers) using that particular type. The first group's steps are notated in bold type, and the second group's will immediately follow in gray type. Before steps for the first group you will see a I, before steps for the second group you will see a II. The two groups should dance these different steps at the same time. (Since the second group's steps are notated in gray type, triplets in this chapter are not notated in gray.)

The combinations given can be performed without music. If you choose to use music, however, it should be in a meter of four, in a duple division and with twelve-bar phrasing. When choreographing the combinations, I used the musical selection "Big Chief" by Professor Longhair.[3]

If you like, combine all the steps in this chapter into one dance for two groups. There is no unison in this dance; so, for contrast, you might want to add unison sections.

At the end of the chapter, I give suggestions for composing your own orchestrated dances.

Rhythmic Canon

We have all experienced canons—for example, when we learned to sing "Row, Row, Row Your Boat" as a group, with some starting later than others. A strict rhythmic canon is like that childhood song. An extended rhythm is repeated exactly by a second part that starts later. We can also make imitative rhythmic canons by layering the original step with a variation.

Remember that, in a variation, some aspect remains the same and some aspect changes. The variation might contain the same steps but have a different timing; it might have different steps but the same rhythm; it might leave out parts of the combination; and so on.

In the beginning of the next dance for two groups (or two people), I have made a six-bar imitative canon, followed by a six-bar strict canon. The first step in the dance is the Extended Time Step described under "Extended Time Step in Duple Time," in Chapter 7. Group II's part is a variation of the Extended Time Step, danced slower with some parts left out.

IMITATIVE RHYTHMIC CANON

		cr	ba		un-cross				travel forward.....................			
	R	L	R	R	L	L	L		R	L	R	L
I.	sc*	hop	br	st	sh-	fl	st		st	st	st	st
	1	2	&	3	&	4	&		(1) &	(2) &	(3) &	(4) &
	>			>					>	>	>	

			cross back to left		
	R	L	R	R	L
II.	sc*	hop	br	st	ST
	1	2	3	4	1	(2)	(3)	(4)
					>
					>

* **Kick right foot and circle it clockwise.**

			L	R	R	R	L	R		L	L	L	R
	R												
I.	STO		STO	sh-	fl	ba-	ch	ST		sh-	fl	ba-	ch
	1	(2)	3	&	4	&	1	&	(2) &	3	&	4
	>		>				>	
			>				>	

	R	L	L	L	R	L			R		L		L	R
II.	STO	sh-	fl	ba-	ch	STO			st		dr		ba-	ch
	1	&	2	&	3	&	(4)	(1)	2		3		4	&
	>				>									
					>									

	to left		in back of L				to left		in back of L				
	L	L	BO	R	R	R	BA	L	L	BO	R	R	R	L
I.	st	hl	cla	br	st	hl	cla	st	hl	cla	br	st	hl	STO
	1	&	2	&	3	&	4	&	1	&	2	&	3	(&)	4
			>				>				>				>

	to left				cr ba to left				
	L	L		L	R				R L BO L
II.	st	hl		hl	st				hl dr cla st
	1	2	(3)	4	1	(2)	(3)		4 & a 1
		>		>					

Strict Rhythmic Canon

The next six bars are a strict canon. The two groups do exactly the same steps, with the second group starting six counts later.

		to right				cr ba of R				fr	ba		
		L	L R BO R			R	L	L	L	R	R		
I.		hl	hl br cla st			hl	br	st	hl	br	br		
	(1)	2	3 & a 4			1	&	2	&	3	&	(4)	(&)
											L		
											hl		
II.	(1)	(2)	(3)	(4)		(1)	(2)	(3)		4			

turn ba clock				continue turning clockwise to front							
R	L R	L		R	R	R	L LR	L	L		L
I. st	st hl	hl*		br	st	hl	3-s-ri	ba	hl		hl
1	& a	2		3	&	4	& . 1	&	2		3 (4)

to right				cr ba of R				fr	ba	turn ba clock			
II. L	R BO	R		R	L	L	L	R	R		R	L R	L
hl	br cla	st		hl	br	st	hl	br	br		st	st hl	hl*
1	& a	2		3	&	4	&	1	&	(2)	3	& a	4

* This is a cramp roll. Do a little jump into the air, landing on the ball of the right foot, then the left. Finish the landing with the two heel-drops.

turn clock once					open	tog			
R		L			R	L	BOTH R L		
I. st	(drag L foot)	STO			st†	st	slide hl	†hl	
1	(2)	3	(4)		1	&	(2) &	3	(4)

continue turning clock to front									
R	R	R	L LR	L	L	L		BO RLRL	
II. br	st	hl	3-s-ri	ba	hl	hl		5 - s - w	
1	&	2	& . . 3	&	4	1	(2)	3 &... 4	

† When done well, this can be a flash step. On the first two steps, straighten the legs and open them, ending with the weight evenly distributed. Open the arms up and out to the side. Extend the slide that brings both legs together for as long as possible, trying to find that magic balance between up and down, to give the impression of weightlessness. As you slide in, bring your arms together and down.

Hocket

Hocket is a technique of composition developed in thirteenth-century medieval music. Meaning "hiccup," it is characterized by quick alternation of two or three parts, with one part resting while the other is sounding. Each part consists of a single note or a short group of notes.[4] This rhythmic interlocking technique has been developed into a fine art in the Gamelon music of Java and has been used in recent years by such avante garde composers as James Tenney, Phillip Glass, and Larry Polansky. In my collaboration with percussionist Gary Schall, we have worked with hockets until we were able to alternate the parts so quickly that, together through alternating notes, we created what sounds like a drum roll.

Continue the dance from where you left off with the following two-part hockets:

	L R R R	R L L L	L R R R	R L L L
I.	hl* br st hl	hl* br st hl	hl* br st hl	hl* br st hl
	4 & a 1	2 & a 3	4 & a 1	2 & a 3

	L R R R	R L L L	L R R R	R L L
II.	hl* br st hl	hl* br st hl	hl* br st hl	hl* br st
	1 & a 2	3 & a 4	1 & a 2	3 & a

turn clockwise

	L R R R	R L L L		R		L	
I.	hl* br st hl	hl* br st hl		st	(drag L)	STO	
	4 & a 1	2 & a 3	(4)	1	(2)	3	(4)

	L	L R R R	R L L L		R		L	
II.	hl	hl* br st hl	hl* br st hl		st	(drag L)	STO	
	4	1 & a 2	3 & a 4	(1)	2	(3)	4	

* **While doing the heel-drop with the left foot, slide the right out to the side like a Fake Wing. Then do the brush step heel toward the left foot, ending with the legs together. Repeat on the other side.**

Repeat the above four measures. Then go to the next step.

		front	front				
		R	L		back R		back L
I.		STO	STO		st		st
		1	2	(3)	&	(4)	&

		front		front	back		back
		R		L	R		L
II.		STO		STO	st		st
	(1)	&	(2)	&	3		4

Repeat three times. Then perform the following break, which is the only unison moment in the dance. Use the walks to change the spacing of the two groups.

	R	L	R	L
I.	walk	walk	walk	walk
	1	2	3	4
	R	L	R	L
II.	walk	walk	walk	walk
	1	2	3	4

Melody Against *Ostinato*

The next example is a two-part rhythm in which a more complex, extended rhythmic phrase (which resembles a melody) is played against a simple repetitive pattern called an "ostinato." Ostinato is commonly used in popular music.

The ostinato phrase that will be used against the extended combination is:

circle R leg		cr	ba								
R		L	R	R		L		R			R
scuff		hop	br	st		st		st			hl
1		2	&	3	(4)	1	(&)	(2)	&	(3)	(&) 4

Alternates sides.

Before you start learning the next combination, you need to know how to do repetitive draw-backs:

R	L	R	L	R	L	
st	dr	hl	st	dr	hl	etc.

Be sure you are fluid in these, both in a triplet and duple rhythm, before learning the complex phrase that follows.

The following extended combination is to be performed by half the group while the other half does the repetitive ostinato rhythm. The first six bars are identical to the beginning of the dance. In the second half of the combination, the spatial instructions are optional.

	cr ba		un-cross				travel forward..........................							
R	L	R	R	L	L	L	R		L		R		L	
sc*	hop	br	st	sh-	fl	st	st		st		st		st	
1	2	&	3	&	4	&	(1)	&	(2)	&	(3)	&	(4)	&
>			>				>		>		>			

* **Kick the right foot and circle it clockwise.**

R		L	R	R	R	L	R	L	L	L	R
STO		STO	sh-	fl	ba-	ch	STO	sh-	fl	ba-	ch
1	(2)	3	&	4	&	1	&	(2)	&	3	&	4
>		>				>						
		>					>					

	to left		in back of L			to left		in back of L					
L	L	BO	R	R	R	BO	L	L	BO	R	R	R	L
st	hl	cla	br	st	hl	cla	st	hl	cla	br	st	hl	STO
1	&	2	&	3	&	4	&	1	&	2	&	3	(&)	4
		>				>			>					>

	face R		turn clockwise			†continue circling until face L									
R		L	L	R	L	R	L	R	L	R	L	R	L
STO		sh-	fl	pb-	ch	Tip	hl	st	dr	hl	st	dr	hl
(1)	(2)	3	(&)	a	4	&	a	1	&	2	&	3	&	4	&
					>			>							

facing L   †circle counterclock until face front

R	R	L	L		R	L	R	L		R	L	R	L	R	L	R	L
db-	le-	fl-	ap‡		hl	hl	hl	hl		st	dr	hl	st	dr	hl	st	st
1		& a	2		3	& a	4			1	&	2	&	3	&	4	&
											>		>			>	>

†circle whole body clockwise one turn until facing front

R		L	R	R	L	R	L	R	L	R	L	R	L	R
scuff*		hop	br	st	dr	hl	st	st	dr	hl	st	dr	hl	ba
1		2	&	3	&	4	&	1	&	2	&	3	&	4
			>			>			>			>		>§

† I use the word "circle" rather than "turn," because you should make a large circle on the floor as you turn, rather than pivoting in one spot.

‡ Flap open with the right foot, then the left foot, while bringing the weight up on to straight legs. End with your weight on both legs and the arms open. During heel-drops, lower your arms and weight.

§ Notice that the accents on the last bar match the rhythm of the ostinato.

Repeat this entire twelve-bar combination with the opposite group doing the *ostinato*.

Rhythmic Counterpoint

The term "rhythmic counterpoint" is often used as a synonym for polyphony. It refers to rhythms created by two or more parts sounding simultaneously. In this book, however, "rhythmic counterpoint" refers to a particular kind of polyphony created by two or more different but equal parts. In other words, counterpoint is created by two dances going on at the same time, thus creating a third, more exciting whole. It is not a canon because the two parts are different. And it is not melody against ostinato because the two parts are equal in complexity.

The following example of rhythmic counterpoint lasts eight bars. The first group dances only the steps in **bold type** while the second group dances the steps in gray type. All of the steps travel, so there are many possibilities of interesting spacial design. Face any directions in the room that you choose. Make steps large to maximize the distance you go.

travel diag forward and to right

	R	R	L	R	R	L	R	R
I.	DG	td	st*	DG	td	st*	st	hl
	1	&	2	&	3	&	4	&
	>			>				

diag forward & R   diag forward & L

	R	L	L	R	L	R	R	L	L
II.	STO	br	st	st	STO	br	st	st	hl
	1	(e)	&	a	2	&	3	&	4	&
	>				>				

travel diag forward and to left

	L	L	R	L	L	R	L	L
I.	DG	td	st*	DG	td	st*	st	hl
	1	&	2	&	3	&	4	&
	>			>				

diag forward & R   diag forward & L

	R	L	L	R	L	R	R	L	L
II.	STO	br	st	st	STO	br	st	st	hl
	1	(e)	&	a	2	&	3	&	4	&
	>				>				

travel diag forward and to right

	R	R	L	R	R	L	R	R
I.	DG	td	st*	DG	td	st*	st	hl
	1	&	2	&	3	&	4	&
	>			>				

*   This is called a catch step. It is a slight leap that replaces the standing leg.

to right side

II.

R	L	L	L	L	R	R	R	R	L	L	L	L	R
STO	dg	dr	st	hl	dg	dr	st	hl	dg	dr	st	hl	ball
1	e	&	a	2	e	&	a	3	e	&	a	4	&
>													>

travel forward

I.

L	L	R		L		R	R	R	L
5	-	s	-	rf		br	st	hl	st*
1	e	&	(a)	2	&	3	&	4	&
>									

travel back

II.

	R	L	L	L	L	R	L
	st	dg	dr	ba†	hl	hl	st
(1)	2	3	e	&	a	4	&
	>	>					>

travel diag forward and to R

I.

R	R	L	R	R	L	R	R
DG	td	st*	DG	td	st*	st	hl
1	&	2	&	3	&	4	&
>		>					

diag forward & R   diag forward & L

II.

R		L	L	R	L	R	R	L	L
STO		br	st	st	STO	br	st	st	hl
1	(e)	&	a	2	&	3	&	4	&
>					>				

* This is called a catch step. It is a slight leap that replaces the standing leg.

† Keep your weight toward the right as you do this fast paddle. After the left ball-tap, keep both feet down on the floor to enable you to do the two heel-drops that follow.

travel diag forward and to left

L	L	R	L	L	R	L	L
DG	td	st*	DG	td	st*	st	hl
1	&	2	&	3	&	4	&

I. accents: > (1), > (col 4 &)

diag forward & R   diag forward & L

R		L	L	R	L	R	R	L	L
STO		br	st	st	STO	br	st	st	hl
1	(e)	&	a	2	&	3	&	4	&

II. accents: > (1), > (&, col 6)

forward; twist body to right

R	L		
st	STO†		
1	2	(3)	(4)

I. accent: > (2)

R	L	L	L	L	R	R	R	R	L	L	L	L	R
STO	dg	dr	st	hl	dg	dr	st	hl	dg	dr	st	hl	ball
1	e	&	a	2	e	&	a	3	e	&	a	4	&

II. accents: > (1), > (&, last)

one counterclockwise turn..

R	L	L		L	R	R	L	R	R
ho	sh-	fl		st	sh-	fl	hop	sh-	fl
1	e	&	(a)	2	&	3	&	4	&

I. accents: > (2), > (&, col 8)

	back							
	R		L	L	L	L	R	L
	st		dg	dr	ba†	hl	hl	st
II. (1)	2		3	e	&	a	4	&
	>		>					>

† Keep your weight toward the right as you do this fast paddle. After the left ball-tap, keep both feet down on the floor to enable you to do the two heel-drops that follow.

Continuation of the Phrase

One dancer continuing the phrase of another is not really polyphony, since there is only one layer of sound; but it is an interesting way, for two dancers or two groups to relate rhythmically.

Below is a four-bar example meant to continue the dance. During the first two bars, the first group begins a phrase, while the second group is still. Then the second group completes the phrase.

	front		back	to right	cr	fr	
	R		L	R	L	L	
I.	st		st	lp	st	hl	(both feet on floor)
	1	(2)	&	(3)	&	4	&

	front			
	R			
	STO (freeze your shape for three counts)			
II.	1	(2)	(3)	(4)

turning clockwise once

	R	L	R	L		L	R	R	R	R	L	L	L	L
I.	hl	td	td	st		hl	dg	dr	st	hl	dg	dr	st	hl
	1	&	2	&		3	e	&	a	4	e	&	a	1

II. (freeze shape for four more counts)

I. (freeze shape for four counts)

L	R	R	R	R	L	L	L	L	R	R	R	R	L	L	L
II. hl	dg	dr	st	hl	dg	dr	st	hl	dg	dr	st	hl	dg	dr	st
1	e	&	a	2	e	&	a	3	e	&	a	4	e	&	a
>				>				>				>			

I. (freeze shape for four more counts)

L	R	R	R	R	R	R	L	L	L	L	L	L	
II. hl	dg	dr	dg	dr	st	hl	dg	dr	dg	dr	st	hl	
1	e	&	a	2	e	&	a	3	e	&	a	4	(&)
>							>					>	

After you have completed the above twelve bars, reverse roles. The first group dances the second group's phrases, and vice versa.

If two groups dance all of the phrases in this chapter with the repetitions, the entire dance is six sets of twelve bars, or a total of seventy-two measures. As I have mentioned, if you use this dance for a performance, intersperse unison sections for contrast. You should also plan exciting spacial designs.

Learning to perform in an orchestrated dance requires much practice. For the counterpoint to be heard, every dancer must be as clear, accurate, and musical as if the dancer were dancing a solo. In the beginning, you'll probably get thrown when you notice the dancer next to you doing a different step. Your goal is to relate visually to the dancers who are in counterpoint and to hear the total effect while dancing.

Now it's time for you to make your own orchestrated combinations. In all the group tap dances I have choreographed over the last twelve years or so, there have been significant orchestrated, or nonunison, sections. In general, I have used two methods to make these sections.

ANITA FELDMAN TAP. Kathryn Tufano, David Parker, Rhonda Price, and Guy Klucevsek, in "City Scraped," by Feldman and Klucevsek. Photo by Tom Caravaglia.

Quite often, I have gotten ideas ahead of time, devised a score, realized the score with the dancers' feet and bodies, and then evaluated the success of what I made by watching and listening.

The time we had the most fun and success working in this way was when I choreographed a piece for three dancers—David Parker, Rhonda Price, and Kathryn Tufano—titled "City Scraped," in collaboration with a new music accordionist, Guy Klucevsek.[5] Guy was interested in the dancers using their voice as an added rhythmic element; but I hadn't yet found a satisfactory way to do that. I had just become pregnant and was instructed firmly by the doctor not to dance. I had one section left to choreograph in the piece, which was to premiere in a month.

The piece so far had been influenced by images of city life—including rushing, waiting, and competing. It was in the middle of the flu season. While commuting, I was struck by the unpleasantness and comedy of everyone coughing and sneezing in such close quarters. I came into rehearsal with a three-part nonunison rhythmic score that included specific counts in which I told each of the three dancers that they had to make an occasional sound toward each other, such as a cough, sneeze, slap, grunt, or exclamation. As the score progressed, the rhythms and sounds became more dense and complex. Each dancer choreographed his or her own phrases, realizing the rhythms that I had composed and using my images and instructions. This section turned out to be the most successful of the piece. The only problem was that, when a dancer really did get a cold during a performance run and she sneezed "off" the beat, the other dancers broke down laughing.

The second way I devise orchestration is by trial and error. We make phrases and hear the result of layering them. We improvise against a set phrase. We experiment with all kinds of canons. I find what I want in the studio by trying many different possibilities, choosing the best and throwing out the rest.

Orchestration Play

1. Work with a partner. Dance any step you have previously learned or made in a strict canon. Try starting four counts apart, six counts apart, eight counts apart. Figure out what works and what doesn't, and why. If you find it difficult to dance and listen at the same time, choreograph on two other dancers or record yourselves.

2. Composer Steve Reich explores the idea of two-part canon fully in his exciting work, "Clapping Music."[6] The piece begins with two musicians clapping the same twelve-count rhythm. The first musician continues to clap this rhythm throughout the entire piece. After twelve repetitions, the second musician shifts the rhythm by one beat, so that count "2" becomes count "1." Every twelve repetitions, the second musician shifts his rhythm by one beat, creating a new canon. This progressive shift of count 1 is called "cycling" or "phas-

ing." Choreograph a simple rhythm that lasts one measure of any length. Have your partner repeat the rhythm. Shift the rhythm progressively by one beat, creating and listening to all the possible canons. Each canon will create a unique, combined rhythm and will require practice.

3. Make three different ostinato patterns. Try them orchestrated with a variety of steps. Once again, figure out what works and what doesn't, and why.

4. Listen to popular music, and find the ostinato patterns. Duplicate the simple rhythm with your feet.

5. Make one four-bar phrase and teach it to a partner. Improvise—one bar at a time while your partner is dancing the set phrase—until you gradually find an accompanying phrase that works well in counterpoint.

6. Notate a four-bar phrase on paper with counts or musical notation. Compose a second phrase on paper that you imagine would work well against the first. After it is composed, realize it with your feet and those of a friend. Does it work?

7. Decide on a simple hocket pattern. Practice it daily with a partner. How fast can you get? Then try adding crescendos and decrescendos.

8. Start with a phrase. Figure out how to dance it twice as fast. Dance the double-time phrase twice against one repetition of the original phrase.

9. Choreograph a phrase that lasts eight bars. Teach it to a partner. Use the following as a score for taking turns continuing the phrase.

1st dancer..2nd dancer..........1st............							
1	2	3	4	1	2	3	4
....2nd dancer...........................							
1	2	3	4	1	2	3	4

............1st..........2nd......................1st.........2nd...........................

| 1 | 2 | 3 | 4 | 1 | 2 | 3 | 4 |

1st dancer.................................2nd dancer............................

| 1 | 2 | 3 | 4 | 1 | 2 | 3 | 4 |

Choreograph how each dancer should move when not dancing.

10. Repeat the above assignment; but this time make your own score. Decide whether you should ever overlap.

11. Below is an excerpt from a score for three tap dancers, entitled "Study for Milwaukee Blues," composed by Larry Polansky for my company. Realize this excerpt for three dancers. Think about both the movement and the sound.

Study for Milwaukee Blues

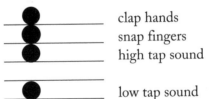

clap hands
snap fingers
high tap sound

low tap sound

IO

New Tap:
Polyrhythms

I WAS STARTING TO WORK ON A NEW PIECE with the composer and percussionist, Gary Schall. He had come to me with a scored rhythm in which he wanted my right foot to tap a simple rhythm mostly in the measure of two, and the left foot to tap a simple rhythm with the same tempo, but in the measure of three. What was exciting—and, at first, seemingly impossible—was that Gary wanted me to do both rhythms at the same time, to create an intriguing whole.

This is just the kind of challenge that sparks my interest. I immediately started to work in the studio, creating a dance phrase to realize the rhythms Gary had scored. At first it was very difficult for me to perform the phrase I had made, but after a little work, the rhythm made sense to me as a whole, and finally it became downright easy.

Here is the rhythm we made:

Left foot: 1   (2)   3   (1)   (2)   (3)   1   (2)   3   (1)   (2)   (3)   1   (2)   (3)

Right foot: (1)   2   (1)   2   (1)   2   (1)   2   (1)   2   (1)   2   (1)   2   (3)

Notated, the two rhythms would look like this:

Left foot: $\| \frac{3}{4} \ \flat \ \flat \ | \ \flat \ \flat \ \flat \ | \ \flat \ \flat \ | \ \flat \ \flat \ \flat \ | \ \flat \ \flat \ \| $

Right foot: $\| \frac{2}{4} \ \flat \ | \ \flat \ | \ \flat \ | \ \flat \ | \ \flat \ | \ \flat \ | \frac{3}{4} \ \flat \ \| $

ANITA FELDMAN TAP. Gary Schall and Anita Feldman, in "Landings," by Feldman and Schall. Photo by Tom Caravaglia.

Try to play this phrase yourself with your right and left feet. Find your own way to use the different parts of your shoe and body movement to make the phrase interesting. Don't get discouraged—with a little time, it will become easy to do.

As a result of my rehearsal session, I had now made a phrase that I liked but that had become too easy. Gary made a suggestion: "Why don't you try changing the left foot's rhythm in any way you want, but keep the right foot's step the same?" Then do the opposite: make the right foot's rhythm different or more complex, and keep the left foot's step the same.

Now I really had an idea to keep me busy for quite a while. In fact, there were so many possibilities that I was able to generate a whole section of a dance work from it. The work was titled "Landings."[1]

Try it yourself! Keep the right foot doing that steady one-two rhythm. Start adding a few sounds to what your left foot is doing. Now you have a whole new phrase. Try it again, adding still more sounds to the left foot.

Then go wild. Totally change your left foot's part, but keep the right foot the same. Choreograph something that interests you. It will take time, but it will be worth it. By giving yourself a challenging rhythmic problem to "solve," you will likely make a new and different rhythmic expression.

I learned later that the term for conflicting rhythms used simultaneously— often as a result of combining different meters at the same time—is "polyrhythm." Another term sometimes used for this is "polymeter."[2] Polyrhythms have been used for centuries in some traditional African music, Balinese music, Brazilian music, and, recently, in avant garde American music. Listen, for instance, to the music of Philip Glass. For additional examples of polyrhythms, refer to the second volume of *Studies in African Music* by A. M. Jones.

Working with polyrhythms opens a whole new world of rhythm. Below are examples of two-part polyrhythms. There are three ways you can play each:

1. Play one part with one foot and the other part with the other foot.
2. Play one part with your feet and one part with your hands.
3. Find a friend and choreograph one part for him or her and one part for you.

I. The top part consists of a step that lasts five counts, repeated three times. The bottom part makes a sound every three counts. (To make it easier to dance, I have counted it in measures of five, however.) The polyrhythm is created by playing a five against a three:

1 & 2 3 (4) 5 1 & 2 3 (4) 5 1 & 2 3 (4) 5

1 (2) (3) 4 (5) (1) 2 (3) (4) 5 (1) (2) 3 (4) (5)

II. The top part makes a sound every four counts, played against the bottom part, which makes a sound every three.

1 (2) (3) (4) 1 (2) (3) (4) 1 (2) (3) (4)

1 (2) (3) 4 (1) (2) 3 (4) (1) 2 (3) (4)

III.   Here is a more difficult variation on the above polyrhythm:

1	(2)	(3)	4 & 1	(2)	(3)	4 & 1	(2)	(3)	4 &

1	(2)	3 & 4	(1)	2 & 3	(4)	1 & 2	(3)	4 &

Following is one possible way to play the above polyrhythm with your right foot against your left:

with R foot

hl			dg* dr st			dg dr st*			DG† td	
1	(2)	(3)	4 & 1	(2)	(3)	4 & 1	(2)	(3)	4 &

with L foot (at the same time)

hl		dg dr st*		dg dr st		dg* dr st		DG† td	
1	(2)	3 & 4	(1)	2 & 3	(4)	1 & 2	(3)	4 &

* In order to step with one foot and dig with the other at the same time, jump into it, landing on the ball of one foot and the heel of the other foot at the same time.

† Jump with both feet on to the back rim of the heels, toe-drop both feet, and then, to repeat the combination, heel-drop both feet.

IV.   Play the following rhythm repetitively with your left foot only:

1 (&) (2) & (3) (&) (4) &

Choreograph a variety of rhythms with your right foot, which you can tap while you are tapping the above rhythm with your left foot. Put these rhythms together to make a dance in which the rhythm of the left foot never changes. It is similar to making an ostinato on the left foot and a melody on the right.

V.   Compose a simple ostinato rhythm for your hands. Choreograph a dance in which the hand rhythm stays constant and the more complicated foot rhythms change their time signature, or change in some other way.

II

New Tap: Unusual and Changing Time Signatures

IN ALL THE TAP DANCE WORKS I have choreographed over the past ten years, I have collaborated with new music composers, including accordionist Guy Klucevsek, software designer David Behrman, percussionist Gary Schall, Lois V Vierk, Larry Polansky, and Michael Kowalski; or I have realized with the dancers' feet percussion scores by Steve Reich and James Tenney. One of the freedoms available to me by creating the music and tap dance through such collaborations is that I can work with measures of unusual length, thereby making new kinds of phrases with my feet. For instance, in a work made with Larry Polansky, entitled *Three Monk Tunes*, the first section, "Bemsha Swing," was composed and danced in measures that lasted seventeen counts.[1]

Following is a short excerpt from "Bemsha Swing." Try choreographing this seventeen-count measure by realizing the tap-dancer rhythms with your feet. The bottom staff is composed for the tap dancer.

clap hands
snap fingers
high tap sound

low tap sound

A co-creation with Lois V Vierk, entitled "Twister," was definitely a mind-twister as well as a body-twister, with movement images suggesting wind and storms and with irregular changes of time signature.[2] Soon after we composed them, these changes became very difficult to remember; but, with practice, the passages became musical and physical, until memory was no longer a problem. As with unusual time signatures, changing time signatures afforded me broader possibilities of rhythmical expression.

Following is an excerpt from the tap part of "Twister." It is composed for a tap dancer, a cellist, and a marimba player. Once again, try this as a choreography assignment. Choreograph a phrase that realizes these tap rhythms in your own way. As an added challenge, you might try to make your phrase turn in unexpected directions, as I did in my choreography.

Collaborating with David Behrman in a work we titled "Hooved Mammals" was a totally new experience, because his music created atmospheres of beautiful sound but had no measures or even a regular underlying beat.[3] I chose to work with David to push myself to create phrases of tap dancing that would not fit into a beat—modern dancers call it "breathe rhythms."

Try it yourself! Choreograph or improvise phrases that give you a particular feeling or image but have no underlying beat. Think of your tapping as a monologue with quickly changing moods—building anger, shyness, hesitation, playfulness, relaxed conversation, and so on.

Anita Feldman in "Twister," by Feldman and Lois V Vierk. Photo by Tom Caravaglia.

The best way to experiment with these musical ideas is to find a musician or composer to work with. If that isn't possible, there are some pieces of music available that have unusual or changing time signatures (see Appendix I).

The best-known works in unusual measures are "Unsquare Dance" in measures of sevens, and "Take Five" in, as you've probably guessed, fives, both by composer Dave Brubeck.[4] To give you a start, I will notate twelve measures of an introduction to a dance that can be performed to "Unsquare Dance." In addition, to give you some practice using your hands in counterpoint with your feet, all the combinations include claps and SLAPS. Wherever you see "SL," it means slap your thigh with your hand or hands. Above the SL, you will see which hand to use or whether to use both hands to make the sound. Whenever I do not instruct you to lift a knee, it means you have to bend over to hit both of your thighs. Continue from where I have left off to choreograph your own original "Unsquare Dance."

*ANITA FELDMAN
TAP. Anita Feldman
and Rhonda Price in
"Hooved Mammals,"
by Feldman and
David Behrman.
Photo by Tom
Caravaglia.*

Hold for the first measure of the music:

				BOTH HANDS SL		
(1)	(2)	(3)	(4)	5	(6)	(7)
				>		

BOTH HANDS clap			BOTH HANDS SL		
(1)	2	(3)	(4)	5	(6)	(7)
	>			>		

R ffflap*	BOTH clap	lift	left knee	BOTH SL†	L step	L hl
1	2	(3)	(4)	5	6	7
	>			>		

Block 1 — "lift R knee" (above beat 5)

1	2	&	3	&	4	&	5	6	7
R	BOTH	L	L	L	R	R	L	R	R
ffflap*	clap	br	st	hl	dg	dr	SL‡	step	hl
	>						>		

Block 2

1	&	2	&	3	&	4	&	5	6	7
L	L	BO	L	L	BO	L	L	BOTH	BOTH	BOTH
dg	dr	cla	dg	dr	cla	st	hl	cla	cla	cla
>		>			>			>	>	>

Block 3

(1)	2	(3)	(4)	5	(6)	(7)
	BOTH			BOTH		
	clap			SL		
	>			>		

Block 4

(1)	2	(3)	(4)	5	(6)	(7)
	BOTH HANDS			BOTH HANDS		
	clap			SL		
	>			>		

Block 5

1	2	(3)	(4)	5	6	7
R	BOTH	lift	left knee	BOTH	L	L
ffflap*	clap			SL†	step	hl
	>			>		

Block 6 — "lift R knee" (above beat 5)

1	2	&	3	&	4	&	5	6	7
R	BOTH	L	L	L	R	R	L	R	R
ffflap*	clap	br	st	hl	dg	dr	SL‡	step	hl
	>						>		

ba,lift	knee	ba.	lift R knee			
L	R	L	L	R	BOTH	R
br	SL‡	lp	SL‡	st	clap	hl
1	2	3	4	5	6	7
	>		>		>	

fr		side		fr		side		fr		ba		fr		front
L	R	BO	R	R	L	BO	L	L	R	BO	R	BO	R	R
st	br	cla	br	st	br	cla	br	st	br	cla	br	cla	st	hl
1	&	2	&	3	&	4	&	5	&	6	&	7	&	1
	>				>					>		>		

* A flat-footed flap is similar to a four-sound riff. Throw your foot down as though you were going to flap, but contact the floor with a very relaxed and almost flat-footed foot. Your goal is to make a roll consisting of four sounds: a ball-tap, scuff, dig, and toe-drop. You accomplish this, not by articulating the foot, but by relaxing and throwing the foot into the sounds. The roll ends on the beat.

† In these SLAPS, hit your lifted knee with both hands, causing that foot to go on to the next step.

‡ In these SLAPS, hit your lifted knee with the opposite hand, causing that foot to go on to the next step. If your right knee is lifted, hit it with the left hand; if your left knee is lifted, hit it with the right hand.

Once you dance the above combination to the music, you will notice that the dance gradually builds until the claps follow the rhythm of the clapping in the music. For your information, "Unsquare Dance" is arranged in phrases that last six measures.

If you can't find a composer or the appropriate music, you have the option of dancing *a capella* (without music). This is very valuable to do, because then you will form your dancing according to your inspiration alone, rather than according to the composer's inspiration. You will then truly be a composer as well as a dancemaker.

12

Tap Futures

TAP DANCE WILL CONTINUE to progress as it has in the past—through the extraordinary ideas and expressions of individuals. There will be as many new futures in tap dance as there are individuals to conceive of them. Maybe one of those new futures will be made by you!

But it will not be the same as it was in tap's golden era, between 1920 and 1934. Then, it was often the tricks of tap dance—who could dance the fastest, who could do back-flips, who could do the most flash steps—and the personality of the dancer (who was the funniest or most unusual, who charmed the audience first) that determined fame and success. In order to be hired by the producers, dancers had to perform surefire crowd-pleasers, often with only a few minutes allotted to them. Despite the fact that audiences adored tap, tap dancing was never the major part of a show.

Today it is the dancemakers who are controlling the entire productions and who will guide the future of tap dance into new directions. The most important new direction is that now choreographers are making dances that develop ideas. The best choreographers are not stringing together steps just because they go with the music or because they must always impress an audience. Rather, dancemakers are developing themes—whether they be rhythmic, expressive or imagistic —into whole forms. And the audiences are responding! In 1989, Steve Condos wrote, "Today, a dancer gets responses from executing a rhythmical phrase, pure rhythm, no tricks! The new 'tricks' are the uses of dynamics, the powerful use of technique, and the blending of rhythms—with or without music—into a unified composition."[1] Choreographers are producing evening-length concerts of tap dance in order to present their ideas adequately.

James "Buster" Brown. Courtesy of Mr. Brown.

Also, choreographers and the audience are developing and perceiving tap dance *as* the music, rather than being *to* the music. Tap dancers have long talked about tap as being music; but now it is really happening. About this subject, Buster Brown wrote, "You've all been coming on to something new without realizing it. You see, instead of just dancing to a tune, now you dance the tune. You're reading the music, playing the note, and giving each note its full value."[2]

The idea of tap dance as music is one that I have particularly explored. By collaborating with composers and composing the tapping as one of the instruments, by using electronics to process the tap sounds, and by inventing the patented "Tap Dance Instrument," a multipitched, acoustic modular floor made of various woods and metal, I have developed tap as an instrument for new music.[3] With her company, the American Tap Dance Orchestra, Brenda Bufalino has focused on the musicality of tap by making complex, nonunison orchestrated works. Many tap choreographers and improvisers—including myself, Brenda Bufalino, Gregory Hines, Fred Strickler, LaVaughn Robinson, and the late Steve Condos—perform entire works without music, so as to bring out the independent musical expression of the tap dance.

Just as the original tap dance grew from a combination of two cultures, Irish and African, unique forms are developing through new blendings of styles of dance and music. Former modern dancers are creating a new form by combining with tap the serious aesthetics, spatial considerations, and the body movement of modern dance. A few of these dancers are Fred Strickler; Lynn Dally, of the Jazz Tap Ensemble; Linda Sohl-Donnell, of Rhapsody in Taps; Heather Cornell, of Manhattan Tap and myself. By combining tap with a variety of music styles— classical, avant garde, rock, and Indian—tap dance has been pushed in new directions. Some tappers, such as Savion Glover and the group Hot Foot are combining tap with the hard edge and raw energy of rap and street dancing.

The future of tap dance can already be seen in all sorts of unexpected places: music festivals of all kinds, colleges, conferences on technology in the arts, modern dance festivals, as well as tap's traditional home—clubs, Broadway, and television. Savion Glover, on Public Television's "Sesame Street," will probably singlehandedly influence millions of children to take up tap dancing.

ANITA FELDMAN TAP. Rhonda Price, Anita Feldman, and David Parker in Hexa, a work by Feldman and Lois V Vierk, which includes electronic processing of the tap dancing on the Tap Dance Instrument. Photo by Daniel Breslin.

On this and the following pages are pictures of some groundbreaking choreographers already mentioned.

Above is a photograph of *Hexa*, created by composer Lois V Vierk and myself, in which, with the use of a digital delay, the dancer's foot rhythms and a percussionist's drumming are magically transformed and layered.

Brenda Bufalino, pictured on the following page, is known for her evening-long, expressive solos as well as her "orchestras," which consist of as many as fifteen dancers.

Brenda Bufalino. Courtesy of The American Tap Dance Orchestra.

Gregory Hines. Courtesy of Gregory Hines and PMK.

Gregory Hines has consistently used his fame to further tap dance by making numerous appearances to benefit other artists. He has forged his own virtuosic solo style of stream of consciousness improvisation.

With his partner Germaine Ingram, LaVaughn Robinson has evolved an intricate, lightning-fast *a capella* duet form.

LaVaughn Robinson. Courtesy of LaVaughn Robinson.

Fred Strickler.
Courtesy of Rhapsody
in Taps. Photo by
Philip Channing.

Fred Strickler's *Tacit Understanding* is a solo that deals with sound, texture, and introspective expression, rather than metered, outgoing rhythms.

The Jazz Tap Ensemble has been touring the world since 1979, as one of the first companies to perform full concerts of original tap dance.

Linda Sohl-Donnell and her percussionist, M. B. Gordy, are pictured in *Piru Bole,* the tap and drum realization of a North Indian rhythmic score composed by John Bergamo.

JAZZ TAP ENSEMBLE. Sam Weber and Derick Grant. Courtesy of Lynn Dally. Photo by Johan Elbers.

RHAPSODY IN TAPS. Linda Sohl-Donnell and M. B. Gordy. Photo by Philip Channing.

Heather Cornell.
Courtesy of Heather
Cornell and
Manhattan Tap.
Photo by Jim Moore.

Heather Cornell combines entertainment with complex structure, as in *Gumbo Hump*, with original music by Ray Brown.

Since the 1960s, many have dreamed of a renaissance of tap dance, where virtuosity is equaled by expression and form.

Now is the time.

Appendix I

Feldman's Favorites: Music Selections with Notes

FOLLOWING IS A TOTALLY SUBJECTIVE LIST of musical choices for dancing and listening.[1] I usually include only one example of each artist or type of music. Finding other recordings by the same artist would expand your musical options. After most listings I have analyzed the selection in terms of division of the beat, length of measures, and phrasing organization.

29 Boogie Woogie, Originaux, RCA Black and White Series, Paris, FSM2 7073.

Probably my choice album for dancing and for listening. Each of the twenty-nine selections is great. Some examples are "Chicago Breakdown," by Big Maceo Merryweather; "Honkey Tonk Train Blues," by Meade "Lux" Lewis; "Yancey's Bugle Call," by Jimmy Yancey; "Boogie Woogie," by Pine Top Smith; and "Cuttin' The Boogie," by Albert Ammons. Although there are some big band selections, most are for solo piano.

For dancing: All selections have a twelve-bar structure, and the beats are divided into triplets. Tempos vary from slow to fast.

---

[1] In order to use musical selections for performance, you must get permission from the artist.

For listening: In the piano works, the left hand usually keeps a steady beat, while the right hand occasionally does some fancy rhythmical play, such as half-time triplets, duple division against the triplet division of the left hand, or a $\frac{3}{4}$ feel against the $\frac{4}{4}$ measure of the left hand.

Thelonious Monk, *The Man I Love,* Black Lion Records, BLP 30141c.

Piano, bass, and drums. Extraordinary, sophisticated rhythms and melodic play. Listen to all selections to hear half-time triplets, changes of tempo within songs, combining duple, triplet, and quadruple division within one song, and more. All selections are wonderful for choreography.

The following selections are rhythmically constant (but none are simple). They can be used for practice and class:

"Ruby My Dear"—very slow; organized in choruses

"Little Rootie Tootie"—moderate triplet flapping tempo; organized in choruses

Professor Longhair, *House Party New Orleans Style, The Lost Sessions 1971– 1972,* 1987; Rounder Records Corporation, Cambridge Mass.

Many selections include singing, but there are a few wonderful instrumental songs:

"Big Chief"—This is the selection I used for the orchestrated tap dance; organized in sections of twelve bars, duple division.

" 'G' Jam"—Organized in sections of twelve bars, jazzy duple division.

"Gone So Long"—Very nice twelve-bar blues, with slow-flapping tempo; triplet division with occasional duple syncopations against the triplet

"501 Boogie"—Reworking of the traditional "Pinetop's Boogie Woogie." Great intricate rhythmic interplay; fast-flapping tempo, triplet division, twelve-bar organization.

Beverly Hills Cop, 1984, MCA Records, MCA.5553.

"Axel F"—An excellent, modern selection. Good for fast Paddle and Rolls; quadruple division with varied phrasing.

Sophisticated Ellington, Duke Ellington and His Orchestra, 1981; New York: RCA Records, CPL2-4098(e); two-record set.

"Perdido"—Slow-moderate flapping tempo; triplet division organized in choruses.

"It Don't Mean A Thing"—With some singing that is in canon (might be fun to dance a canon with it); moderate-fast flapping tempo, triplet division organized in choruses.

"Do Nothin' Till You Hear From Me"—Nice soft shoe tempo; slow triplet division with varied phrasing.

"The Mooche"—Slow-moderate flapping tempo; triplet division organized in choruses.

"Take The 'A' Train"—A tap classic; moderate flapping tempo, triplet division organized in choruses.

"Rockin' in Rhythm"—Fun moderate-fast flapping tempo; triplet division organized in choruses with occasional unpredictable exceptions.

"Dancers in Love"—One of my favorites: fast flapping tempo, triplet division organized in choruses.

"Don't Get Around Much Anymore"—Soft shoe tempo; slow triplet division organized in choruses.

Preservation Hall Jazz Band, New Orleans, Vol. III; New York: CBS, Inc., 1983; FMT 38650.

"Hindustan"—Very fast, flapping tempo; triplet division organized in choruses.

"Bye and Bye"—Fast flapping tempo; triplet division organized in choruses.

"Just a Closer Walk with Thee"—Slow soft shoe tempo; very slow triplet division organized in choruses.

Gershwin Plays Gershwin, The Piano Rolls, 1993; Elektra Entertainment, 79287-2.

"Kickin' the Clouds Away"—Wonderful moderate flapping tempo with interludes of duples, great for understanding and experiencing the difference between triplets and duples; organized in choruses with some exceptions.

"Idle Dreams"—Interesting duple divisioned music that has frequent rubato. In other words, the tempo slightly slows and quickens frequently, good for choreography and listening.

"On My Mind The Whole Night Long"—Fast flapping tempo; triplet division organized in choruses with some exceptions.

Dave Brubeck's All-Time Greatest Hits, New York: CBS, Inc., 1974; PG32761.

The entire two album set is great to study for its complex rhythms, but the following are my favorite songs for dancing:

"Take Five"—Wonderful song with a $\frac{5}{4}$ time signature; fast tempo, duple division organized in choruses.

"Unsquare Dance"—Great song in $\frac{7}{4}$ time signature; duple division organized in phrases of six measures.

"It's a Raggy Waltz"—Complex $\frac{3}{4}$ time signature in which intermittently the drum keeps the $\frac{3}{4}$ Time, and the other instruments do a $\frac{2}{4}$ time against it. This technique is called a "Hemiola." It's marvelous!

"My Favorite Things"—Fast $\frac{3}{4}$ time signature with some fancy variations in the melody; duple division organized in choruses.

"Blue Rondo a la Turk"—With measure lengths of nine, the opening is exciting and challenging; the counts are grouped as follows: 2-2-2-3, 2-2-2-3, 2-2-2-3, 3-3-3, great for listening or for the advanced, adventuresome dancer.

Scott Joplin, *Piano Rags*, Joshua Rifkin, piano; Nonesuch Records, 1970; H-71248.

In general, ragtime is good music for duple or quadruple division steps.

"Maple Leaf Rag"—Moderate tempo duple division, great for Paddle and Roll and its variations; organized in choruses.

"The Entertainer"—Slow tempo duple division; organized in choruses.

"The Ragtime Dance"—moderate tempo duple division, great for Paddle and Roll and its variations; organized in choruses.

"Fig Leaf Rag"—Slow tempo, duple division; organized in choruses.

"Scott Joplin's New Rag"—Fast-moderate tempo duple division; organized in choruses.

"Magnetic Rag"—Slow-moderate tempo duple division; organized in choruses.

The Complete Glenn Miller, Vol. II, 1939; New York: RCA Records, 1976; AXM2-5514.

"Glen Island Special"—Fast duple division, organized in choruses; great for fast Paddle and Roll.

"In the Mood"—A tap dance staple: moderate flapping tempo, triplet division, for the most part organized in twelve bars.

Jay Clayton, *All-Out,* c1981, Anima Productions, New York, NY.

Jay Clayton is an unusual and extraordinary scat singer. All selections are great for study and choreography. The following are also possible to use for class or practice:

"Random Mondays"—Slow duple division; you must listen carefully to keep the beat throughout the piece.

"$\frac{7}{8}$ Thing"—Very beautiful mellow piece in $\frac{7}{8}$ time signature.

Lennie Pickett with the Borneo Horns, Ryko Disk, 1987; CGLP 7001.

Lennie Pickett is a new music saxophonist who makes wonderfully rhythmic and lively pieces that are great for listening and dancing. This CD or cassette is played by three saxophonists and a drummer.

Four Dancing Masters, featuring Jimmy Slyde, Baby Laurence, Bunny Briggs, Chuck Green; produced by Black and Blue, Paris, 33.165 WE341.

These four tap dance legends are recorded dancing to some wonderful jazz music selections. Listen and dance to it for the musical selections, and listen to the tap for inspiration and education.

The Smithsonian Collection of Classic Jazz, Smithsonian Institution, 1973. Distributed by W.W. Norton, Washington D.C., P611891-11897.

This collection contains a wealth of previously issued recordings of popular jazz and blues music by various artists. One source for buying parts of this collection is The American Tap Dance Orchestra, 799 Broadway, Suite 422, New York, NY 10003.

TAPES MADE RECENTLY FOR TAP DANCE

Ten Tunes for Tap, 1990; DoBe Productions, P.O. Box 5443, Denver, Colorado 80217.

A variety of types of original selections made with a synthesizer and best used for class and practice. My favorites are:

"Taps And Drums"—Fancy drum rhythms alternating with Stop-time, great for practice in listening and improvising; triplet division organized in choruses.

"Waltz"—Not the most interesting of waltzes; but, since jazz waltzes are hard to find, I'm including it; $\frac{3}{4}$ time organized in choruses.

"African Poly-rhythms"—Drumming that keeps a steady tempo but has changing and unusual time signatures; great to analyze and then choreograph to.

"Earth Day Boogie"—Great Boogie Woogie, moderate flapping tempo, with some Stop-time, twelve-bar structure, triplet division.

"In a Family Way"—Modern song great for moderately tempoed Paddle and Rolls, quadruple division organized in choruses.

Music for Tap. Produced by Sam Weber, 1433 Yale St., #B1, Santa Monica, CA 90404, in collaboration with Jerry Kalaf and musicians of the Jazz Tap Ensemble.

Recording of danceable, somewhat mellow jazz standards arranged specifically for tap, with Stop-time. Good for class and practice.

My favorites:

"Oleo"—A be-bop tune in which the melody rides over the measures, causing interesting syncopations, good for listening and dancing. It is recorded in two tempoes, triplet division organized in choruses.

"Green Dolphin Street"—Interesting because it switches off several times between jazzy triplet division sections and Latin duple division sections.

"Someday My Prince Will Come"—Lyrical $\frac{3}{4}$ time signature with some complex rhythmic interplay between the melody and the underlying beat.

The following are swing music, big band song selections great for tap, which you could find on many albums. Most are at a moderate or fast flapping tempo in triplet division:

Benny Goodman: "Flyin' Home," "Sing Sing Sing" (a great tap song!), "Fascinatin' Rhythm," "Honeysuckle Rose."

Count Basie Band: "One O'Clock Jump"; "Blues with Lips"; "I Ain't Got Nobody" (nice slow tempo that switches to double-time); "Cute."

Les Brown: "Leap Frog."

Tommy Dorsey: "Song of India."

Fats Waller: "The Jitterbug Waltz" (solo piano).

teach you the Buggy Ride sentences, we start many of the Time Steps on the upbeat before count 1.

    7. Refer to Chapter 8 for detailed instructions on a Fake Wing.

    8. Refer to Chapter 8 for detailed instruction on a Five-Sound Wing.

CHAPTER 8

    1. Marshall and Jean Stearns, *Jazz Dance* (New York: Macmillan, 1968), pp. 125, 190.

    2. "The Jazz Hoofer: The Story of the Legendary Baby Lawrence," directed and produced by Bill Hancock (New York: Rhapsody Films, 1981.)

    3. Stearns, *Jazz Dance*, p. 193.

    4. Some tappers swing the arms in opposition, but I prefer this method.

    5. Refer to p. 143 for detailed instructions on a Fake Wing.

CHAPTER 9

    1. Richard Kislan, *Hoofing on Broadway* (New York: Prentice-Hall Press, 1987), p. 55.

    2. Willi Appel and Ralph T. Daniel, *The Harvard Brief Dictionary of Music* (New York: Washington Square Press, 1960), p. 229.

    3. "Big Chief" can be found in many Professor Longhair albums, including: *House Party New Orleans Style; The Lost Sessions 1971-1972* (1987, Rounder Records Corporation, Cambridge, Mass.).

    4. Appel and Daniel, *The Harvard Brief Dictionary of Music*, p. 135.

    5. "City Scraped" (1991) was choreographed by Anita Feldman with creative contributions by David Parker, Rhonda Price and Kathryn Tufano, with music composed by Guy Klucevsek. Funding was provided by Meet the Composer and the National Endowment for the Arts.

    6. Steve Reich, "Clapping Music" (London: Universal Edition, 1980), UE 16182 L.

CHAPTER 10

    1. "Landings" (1989) was choreographed and composed by Anita Feldman and Gary Schall in 1989, with funding from a 1989 National Endowment for the Arts Choreography Fellowship.

    2. Willi Appel and Ralph T. Daniel, *The Harvard Brief Dictionary of Music* (New York: Washington Square Press, 1960), p. 230.

CHAPTER 11

    1. "Three Monk Tunes" (1985) was choreographed by Anita Feldman and composed by Larry Polansky.

    2. "Twister" (1993) was co-created by Anita Feldman and Lois V Vierk with funding from Meet the Composer's Composer/Choreographer Project.

    3. "Hooved Mammals" (1992 and 1993) was co-created by Anita Feldman and David Behrman with creative contributions by Rhonda Price and Vera Huff, with funding from the Mary Flagler Cary Charitable Trust, and the National Endowment for the Arts.

    4. Dave Brubeck, *Dave Brubeck's All-Time Greatest Hits* (New York: Columbia Records, 1974), PG32761.

CHAPTER 12

    1. Steve Condos, "The Way I See It," *International Tap Association Journal*, vol. 2, no. 1 (Fall 1989), p. 19.

2. Constance Valis Hill, "What's New in Tap . . . or Should I Ask?" *International Tap Association Journal*, vol. 3, no. 1(Spring/Summer 1991), p. 4.

3. For more information about my Tap Dance Instrument (patent #4,955,276), refer to the *International Tap Association Journal*, vol. 1, no. 2 (February 1989), pp. 8-9.

Index

Page numbers in italics indicate illustrations

a capella, 9, 186
Ability, creative versus technical, 17
Accents, xii, 45, 48, 57, 59, 67, 85, 86, 88, 163
American Tap Dance Orchestra, 191
Ammons, Albert, 199
Anita Feldman Tap, 84, 192
Astaire, Fred, 12, 13, 14
Atkins, Cholly, 9

Ball-change, xiii
Ball-tap, xiii, xv, 94, 96, 110, 139, 165, 167, 186
Beat, 4, 40
  subdivisions, 3
  syncopating, 65
  underlying, 37, 38, 46, 51
Behrman, David, 181, 182, 184
Bemsha Swing, 181
Bennett, David, 155
Bergamo, John, 196
Berkeley, Busby, 155
"Big Chief," 156, 200
Body movement, xxii
Break, 29, 31, 108

Demand a, 30
Time Step, 30
two-bar, 9
Briggs, Bunny, 204
Brown, James "Buster," *190*, 191
Brown, King Rastus, 7, 14
Brown, Ralph, 14
Brown, Ray, 198
Brubeck, Dave, 183, 202
Brush Step, xiii, 141, 160
Bryant, Willie, 105
Bubbles, John, 9, 14, 65
Buck dancing, 7, 111
Bufalino, Brenda, 191, *193*
Buffalo (dance step), 51
Buggy Ride Time Step, 50
  Double, 113
  Double-Triple, 113
  Single, 112
  Triple, 113
  Triple-Triple, 114
Bumbishay, xiii, 122
Bumbishay Break in Fives, 123
Bumbishay Time Step in a Measure of Five, 122
"By Word of Foot," 9

Canon, Rhythmic, 156
  Imitative Rhythmic, 157
  Strict Rhythmic, 158
Capezio Teletone Taps, 2
Catch step, 167
Chug, xiii, 70, 120, 14
  flap, 120
Chug Break, 120
Chug Step Break, 120
Cincinatti (dance step), 51
"City Scraped," *169*
Clapping Variation, 121
Clayton, Jay, 204
Cleats, 2
Click, xiii
Clog, traditional waltz, 66
Coles, Honi, 9, 75
Condos, Frank, 9, 127
Condos, Steve, 9, *10*, 11, 189,
  191
Connie's Inn, 106
Cornell, Heather, 191, *198*
Count Basie Band, 206
Counterpoint, rhythmic, 163,
  168, 183
Counting versus rhythmic
  feeling, 37
Counts, xii
Cramp Roll, xiv, 45, 93, 159
Cramp Roll Time Step, 115
Crawl, xiv, 91, 95, 102;
  one-legged, 91, 95
  two-legged, 92, 93
Crawl combinations, 94
Crescendo, xii, 59
Cross back, xx
Cross front, xx
Cross-Over, 106

Dally, Lynn, 191
Dance
  ballroom, 13
  flash, 128
  jazz, 1
  orchestrated, 168
  percussive, 9
  tap, 13
  Trading Eights, 33
Dance speed, 102
"Darktown Follies," 127
Davis, Toots, 127
Decrescendo, xii, xiv, 59
Division, duple: see Duple division.
Division, quintuplet: see Quintu-
  plet division.
Division, triplet: see Triplet divi-
  sion.
Donohue, Jack, 13, 111
Dorsey, Tommy, 206
Downbeat, 42, 46, 47, 79, 210
Draper, Paul, xxii, 13
Draw-back, xiv, xviii, 96, 161
Drum machine, 44, 76
Duple division, 21, 40-41, 43-44,
  47, *67*, 68-69, 72, *85*, 96-99,
  112, 116-117, 156, 161, 200
Dynamics, xii, 48, 55, 56, 57, 59,
  62-63

Easter Parade, 13
Ellington, Duke, 201

"Falling Off a Log" (step), 107
Feldman, Anita, *101, 176, 183, 184*
Flap, xv, 132
  Double, xiv, 134
  Flat-footed, xiv, 186

Flaps, running, 38
Flash steps, 127-128, 144
Floor finishes, 207
Floors, 2-4, 207; tap, xxi
"Follow the Leader," 19-20
Forte, xii, 55
Fortissimo, xii, 55

Games, improvisation, 17-18
    mutation, 22
Glass, Phillip, 159, 177
Glenn Miller, The Complete, 203
Glover, Savion, 191
Goodman, Benny, 206
"Goofus," 105, 106
Gordy, M.B., 196, *197*
Gould, Morton, 52
Grace notes, xii
Grant, Derick, *197*
Green, Chuck, 204

Half Break Step, *107*, 108
Heel, double-flap, 120
Heel drop, xv, 62, 82, 94, 160, 163
Hexa, *192*
Hicks, Lonnie, 14
Hines, Gregory, 16, 19, 191, *194*
Hocket, the, 159, 160
Honolulu, 14
"Hoofers," 11
Hoofers Club, The, 14
"Hooved Mammals," 182, *184*
Hop, xv, 147
Hot Foot group, 191

Improvisation, 16-18, 21, 33
Ingram, Germaine, 194

Jazz, 65, swinging, 65
Jazz dance, 13
Jazz Tap Ensemble, *197*
Jazz music, 38, 43
Jazz Step, 108, 110
Jazz Tap Ensemble, 191, 196
Jones, Joe, 106
Jones, A. M., 177
Joplin, Scott, 51, 203
Jump, xv

King, Mattie, 127
Kirn, Marda, 16
Klucevsek, Guy, *169*, 181
Kowalski, Michael, 181
Land, xv
"Landings," *176*
Lawrence, Baby, 14, 127, 204
Leap, xv
Lewis, Meade "Lux," 51, 199
"Little Rootie Tootie," 38, 200

Manhattan Tap, 191
"Maxi Ford," 49
Maxi Ford rhythm, 50
Measures, 38, 43
Metronome, 44, 76
Mezzoforte, xii, 55
Mezzopiano, xii, 56
Monk, Thelonius, 38, 51, 200
Morton, Jelly Roll, 51
Music, polyphonic, 156
Music notation, xii, 39
Music
    funk, 65
    Gamelon, 15

Hawaiian, 14
jazz, 38, 43
popular, 38
rock, 44
Mutation games, 22
Mutation variations, 24
Mutations
  demanding, 23
  memory, 2
  solo, 22
  telephone, 23

National Tap Dance Day, 9
"Next Step, The," 31
Notation, musical, xi, xii, 39
Note, eighth, 40

Orchestation, 170
Ostinato: melody against, 161
Ostinato Trading Eights, 32
Ostinato pattern, 32
"Outlaw style," 13
Over the Top, xv, 127, *129,* 130-132
Over the Top Combination with Time Step, 149

Paddle and Roll, xvi, 47-48, 51, 57, 84, 86, 102
  Double, xiv
  Triple, xvii, 88
Paddle Combo, 90
Parker, David, 169, *192*
Phrase play
  completing, 28
  contracting, 26
  dynamic, 29
  expanding, 27
  guess the, 29
Phrasing, 43
Pianissimo, 55, 56
Piano
  instrument, 56
  dynamics, 55
Piano Rags, 202
Pickett, Lennie, 204
Piru Bole, 196
Pivot, counterclockwise, 71
Polansky, Larry, 159, 172, 181
Polyphony, 156, 163, 167
Polyrhythms, 177, 178
Powell, Eleanor, 13-14
Practice, solo, xxi
Preservation Hall Jazz Band, 201
Price, Rhonda, 169, *184,* 192
Professor Longhair, 156, 200
Pullback, xvi, 50, 132-134
  Double, xiv, 134
  One-Legged, 135, 136
  Single, 133
Pullback change, xvi
Pullback Combination, Changeover, 147
Pullback Change, in Triplets, Turn with, 151
Pulling the Trenches, 127, 131

Quad division, 22, 40, 42, 71, 100
Quarter note, 38
Quintuplet division, 100

Ragtime, 51
Rap Tap, 26
Reed, Leonard, 14, 105
Reich, Steve, 170, 181

Appendix II

Product Suggestions

PORTABLE FLOORS

Rusty Frank Tap Mat, a roll-out portable mat of any size, is sold by On Tap: 8565 Chalmers Drive, #2, Los Angeles, CA 90035; phone: 310-657-7664.

FLOOR FINISHES

Two sealers for wood floors are Tung Oil and Watco Oil. Both oils strengthen the floor while also sealing it from water damage and warping. Be sure to follow the directions on the container, wiping the excess oil off before allowing it to dry.

Another option is nonglossy polyurethane varnish, which is tougher than oil.

If the wood floor is too slippery, try Slip Nomor and water according to directions on the label. It is sold through Stage Step, Philadelphia, Pennsylvania: 1-800-523-0961 or 1-215-829-9800.

Tap Shoes

Men's Capezio Tap Shoe. Taps and rubber must be bought separately.

The Gregory Hines Tap Shoe from Capezio. Sold ready to tap for men and women.

The Dansky Shoe. Designed by Brenda Bufalino and Avi Miller and sold

Notes

INTRODUCTION

1. For specific product suggestions, refer to Appendix II.
2. Paul Draper, "Look or Listen," *Dance Magazine* (March 1962), p. 73.

CHAPTER 1

1. Refer to Appendix II for product suggestions.
2. Refer to Appendix II for product suggestions.
3. Dan Peterson, "Floors for Dance," *Dance Research Annual X*, ed. Patricia A. Rowe and Ernestine Stodelle (Congress on Research in Dance, 1979), pp. 95-114.
4. Refer to Appendix II for product suggestions.
5. Raoul Gelabert, "Dance Floors: Their Selection and Preparation," *Dance Magazine* (March 1972), pp. 94-95.

CHAPTER 2

1. Marshall and Jean Stearns, *Jazz Dance* (New York: Macmillan, 1968), pp. 186–187.
2. Noel Carroll, "Review: By Word of Foot," *Dance Magazine* (January 1981), p. 96.
3. "A capella" means "without accompanying music."
4. From a phone interview with Condos's wife, Lorraine, November 27, 1994.
5. From workshops and conversations with Steve Condos at the Colorado Dance Festival and in New York City, 1989-1990.
6. Rusty E. Frank, *Tap!* (New York: William Morrow, 1990), pp. 231-237.
7. Stearns, *Jazz Dance*, p. 226.
8. Ibid., p. 224.
9. Tony Thomas, *That's Dancing!* (New York: Harry Abrams, 1984).
10. Ibid.
11. Stearns, *Jazz Dance*, pp. 338, 173.
12. Marshall and Jean Stearns, *Jazz Dance* (New York: Macmillan, 1968), p. 177.
13. An ostinato is a clearly defined melodic or rhythmic phrase that is persistently repeated throughout a piece of music.

14. It is not advisable to use rhythms from copyrighted scores for professional performance without permission.

CHAPTER 3

1. There are many books that provide detailed training in reading musical notation. Two that I suggest are *Basic Rhythmic Training* and *Rhythmic Training*, both by Robert Starer. Published by MCA Music Publishing, New York, they provide clear explanations and numerous wonderful rhythms.

2. Thelonious Monk, "Little Rootie Tootie," *The Man I Love*, Black Lion Records, BLP30141c.

3. Running flaps are brush steps that alternate feet, performed with easily bent knees, like an easy jog in place.

4. For more information on unusual and changing lengths of measures, see Chapter 11.

5. A downbeat is the first beat of the measure.

6. For more information on accents and the notation for accents, refer to Chapter 4, "Dynamics."

7. Be sure to get permission from the composer if you use a rhythm from a copyrighted score for professional performance.

8. Once again, you must get permission to use rhythms for professional performance.

CHAPTER 4

1. Internationally agreed upon musical terms are usually in Italian.

2. Willi Appel and Ralph T. Daniel, *The Harvard Brief Dictionary of Music* (New York: Washington Square Press, 1960), p. 2.

3. A "Break" is a step that is different from the repeated pattern that precedes it. The Break usually completes the phrase.

CHAPTER 5

1. Ted Reed, *Progressive Steps to Syncopation for the Modern Drummer* (Clearwater, FL: ***, 1958)

CHAPTER 6

1. Stop-time is an interlude in the music in which only a simple rhythm is played to hold the tempo, allowing the tap dancer to solo.

2. Trina Marx, *Tap Dance* (Englewood Cliffs, N.J.: Prentice-Hall, 1983), p. 60; Marshall and Jean Stearns, *Jazz Dance* (New York: Macmillan, 1968), p. 306.

3. Stearns, *Jazz Dance*, p. 351.

4. "Takeoff" was choreographed in 1992, by Anita Feldman, in collaboration with percussionist Gary Schall with funding from a 1991 National Endowment for the Arts Choreography Fellowship.

CHAPTER 7

1. Phone interview with Rusty Frank, November 30, 1994; and Frank, *Tap!* (New York: William Morrow, 1990), pp. 43–44.

2. Marshall and Jean Stearns, *Jazz Dance* (New York: Macmillan, 1968), p. 196.

3. For instructions on performing Over-the-Tops, refer to Chapter 7, Flash Steps.

4. Taught to me by Lynne Jassem.

5. Jack Donohue, "Hoofing," *Saturday Evening Post* (September 14, 1929).

6. Traditional Time Steps often begin with the Stamp, dig, or shuffle on count 4; but, in order to

teach you the Buggy Ride sentences, we start many of the Time Steps on the upbeat before count 1.

7. Refer to Chapter 8 for detailed instructions on a Fake Wing.

8. Refer to Chapter 8 for detailed instruction on a Five-Sound Wing.

CHAPTER 8

1. Marshall and Jean Stearns, *Jazz Dance* (New York: Macmillan, 1968), pp. 125, 190.

2. "The Jazz Hoofer: The Story of the Legendary Baby Lawrence," directed and produced by Bill Hancock (New York: Rhapsody Films, 1981.)

3. Stearns, *Jazz Dance*, p. 193.

4. Some tappers swing the arms in opposition, but I prefer this method.

5. Refer to p. 143 for detailed instructions on a Fake Wing.

CHAPTER 9

1. Richard Kislan, *Hoofing on Broadway* (New York: Prentice-Hall Press, 1987), p. 55.

2. Willi Appel and Ralph T. Daniel, *The Harvard Brief Dictionary of Music* (New York: Washington Square Press, 1960), p. 229.

3. "Big Chief" can be found in many Professor Longhair albums, including: *House Party New Orleans Style; The Lost Sessions 1971–1972* (1987, Rounder Records Corporation, Cambridge, Mass.).

4. Appel and Daniel, *The Harvard Brief Dictionary of Music*, p. 135.

5. "City Scraped" (1991) was choreographed by Anita Feldman with creative contributions by David Parker, Rhonda Price and Kathryn Tufano, with music composed by Guy Klucevsek. Funding was provided by Meet the Composer and the National Endowment for the Arts.

6. Steve Reich, "Clapping Music" (London: Universal Edition, 1980), UE 16182 L.

CHAPTER 10

1. "Landings" (1989) was choreographed and composed by Anita Feldman and Gary Schall in 1989, with funding from a 1989 National Endowment for the Arts Choreography Fellowship.

2. Willi Appel and Ralph T. Daniel, *The Harvard Brief Dictionary of Music* (New York: Washington Square Press, 1960), p. 230.

CHAPTER 11

1. "Three Monk Tunes" (1985) was choreographed by Anita Feldman and composed by Larry Polansky.

2. "Twister" (1993) was co-created by Anita Feldman and Lois V Vierk with funding from Meet the Composer's Composer/Choreographer Project.

3. "Hooved Mammals" (1992 and 1993) was co-created by Anita Feldman and David Behrman with creative contributions by Rhonda Price and Vera Huff, with funding from the Mary Flagler Cary Charitable Trust, and the National Endowment for the Arts.

4. Dave Brubeck, *Dave Brubeck's All-Time Greatest Hits* (New York: Columbia Records, 1974), PG32761.

CHAPTER 12

1. Steve Condos, "The Way I See It," *International Tap Association Journal*, vol. 2, no. 1 (Fall 1989), p. 19.

2. Constance Valis Hill, "What's New in Tap . . . or Should I Ask?" *International Tap Association Journal,* vol. 3, no. 1(Spring/Summer 1991), p. 4.

3. For more information about my Tap Dance Instrument (patent #4,955,276), refer to the *International Tap Association Journal,* vol. 1, no. 2 (February 1989), pp. 8-9.

Index

Page numbers in italics indicate illustrations

a capella, 9, 186
Ability, creative versus technical, 17
Accents, xii, 45, 48, 57, 59, 67, 85, 86, 88, 163
American Tap Dance Orchestra, 191
Ammons, Albert, 199
Anita Feldman Tap, 84, 192
Astaire, Fred, 12, 13, 14
Atkins, Cholly, 9

Ball-change, xiii
Ball-tap, xiii, xv, 94, 96, 110, 139, 165, 167, 186
Beat, 4, 40
  subdivisions, 3
  syncopating, 65
  underlying, 37, 38, 46, 51
Behrman, David, 181, 182, 184
Bemsha Swing, 181
Bennett, David, 155
Bergamo, John, 196
Berkeley, Busby, 155
"Big Chief," 156, 200
Body movement, xxii
Break, 29, 31, 108

Demand a, 30
Time Step, 30
two-bar, 9
Briggs, Bunny, 204
Brown, James "Buster," *190*, 191
Brown, King Rastus, 7, 14
Brown, Ralph, 14
Brown, Ray, 198
Brubeck, Dave, 183, 202
Brush Step, xiii, 141, 160
Bryant, Willie, 105
Bubbles, John, 9, 14, 65
Buck dancing, 7, 111
Bufalino, Brenda, 191, *193*
Buffalo (dance step), 51
Buggy Ride Time Step, 50
  Double, 113
  Double-Triple, 113
  Single, 112
  Triple, 113
  Triple-Triple, 114
Bumbishay, xiii, 122
Bumbishay Break in Fives, 123
Bumbishay Time Step in a Measure of Five, 122
"By Word of Foot," 9

Canon, Rhythmic, 156
  Imitative Rhythmic, 157
  Strict Rhythmic, 158
Capezio Teletone Taps, 2
Catch step, 167
Chug, xiii, 70, 120, 14
  flap, 120
Chug Break, 120
Chug Step Break, 120
Cincinatti (dance step), 51
"City Scraped," *169*
Clapping Variation, 121
Clayton, Jay, 204
Cleats, 2
Click, xiii
Clog, traditional waltz, 66
Coles, Honi, 9, 75
Condos, Frank, 9, 127
Condos, Steve, 9, *10*, 11, 189,
  191
Connie's Inn, 106
Cornell, Heather, 191, *198*
Count Basie Band, 206
Counterpoint, rhythmic, 163,
  168, 183
Counting versus rhythmic
  feeling, 37
Counts, xii
Cramp Roll, xiv, 45, 93, 159
Cramp Roll Time Step, 115
Crawl, xiv, 91, 95, 102;
  one-legged, 91, 95
  two-legged, 92, 93
Crawl combinations, 94
Crescendo, xii, 59
Cross back, xx
Cross front, xx
Cross-Over, 106

Dally, Lynn, 191
Dance
  ballroom, 13
  flash, 128
  jazz, 1
  orchestrated, 168
  percussive, 9
  tap, 13
  Trading Eights, 33
Dance speed, 102
"Darktown Follies," 127
Davis, Toots, 127
Decrescendo, xii, xiv, 59
Division, duple: see Duple division.
Division, quintuplet: see Quintu-
  plet division.
Division, triplet: see Triplet divi-
  sion.
Donohue, Jack, 13, 111
Dorsey, Tommy, 206
Downbeat, 42, 46, 47, 79, 210
Draper, Paul, xxii, 13
Draw-back, xiv, xviii, 96, 161
Drum machine, 44, 76
Duple division, 21, 40-41, 43-44,
  47, *67*, 68-69, 72, *85*, 96-99,
  112, 116-117, 156, 161, 200
Dynamics, xii, 48, 55, 56, 57, 59,
  62-63

Easter Parade, 13
Ellington, Duke, 201

"Falling Off a Log" (step), 107
Feldman, Anita, *101, 176, 183, 184*
Flap, xv, 132
  Double, xiv, 134
  Flat-footed, xiv, 186

Rests, 40-41
Rhapsody in Taps, 191, *197*
Rhythm tap, 9, 21, 155
"Rhythm turn," 62
Rhythms, "breathe," 182
Riffs, xvi, 95, 102
Riff
  advanced, 99
  3-sound, xviii, 95, 97
  3-sound-reverse, xviii
  4-sound, xviii, 96, 186
  4-sound-reverse, xviii, 9
  5-sound, xviii, 96
  5-sound-reverse, xviii, 97
  7-sound, xviii, 96
  7-sound-reverse, xviii, 97
Riff Combo
  Advanced, 102
  Duple Division, 99
Riffle, xvi, 96, 100, 102
  Reverse, 97
Robinson, Bill "Bojangles," 7, 9, 14
Robinson, LaVaughn, 19, *191*, 194, *195*
Rock music, 44, 191
Rosalie, 14
Royal Wedding, 13

"Scat" singing, xxi
Schall, Gary, 31, *101*, 160, 175, *176*, 181
Scuff, xvi, 95
"Sesame Street," 191
Shim Sham, 106
Shim Sham Break, 106
Shim Sham Club, 106
Shim Sham Combination with

Over the Top, 150
Shim Sham Shimmy, 105, 106, 108, 111
Shoes, 207
  as musical instrument, 1
Shuffle, xvi, 77
  crossing, 67
  Double, xiv, 79, 80
  flat-footed, 7
  Single, 78
Shuffle Combo, 83
Shuffle string, xvi, 79
Shuffle Off to Buffalo, 48-49
Slap, xvii, 183, 186
Slide, xvii
Slyde, Jimmy, *15*, 16, 204
Smith, Pine Top, 199
Smithsonian Collection of Classic Jazz, 204
Soft Shoe, 30, 51
Sohl-Donnell, Linda, 191, 196, *197*
Stamp, xvii, 56
Step
  catch, 167
  flash, 127
  flat-footed, 7
  traditional tap, 13
"Steps, stealing," 14
Stick Control for the Snare Drummer, 52
Stomp, xvii
Stone, George Lawrence, 52
Stop-time, 75
Strickler, Fred, 191, *196*
Studies in African Music, 177
"Study for Milwaukee Blues," 172

Style, developing, 17
Suzie Q, 108, 109
Suzie Q Break, 110
Swing Time, 13
Swing, 9
Symbols used, xii, xx
Syncopation, 65, 68, 73

Tacit Understanding, 196
Tack Annie, 107
"Takeoff," *101*
Tap (movie), 16
Tap Dance, vii, 7, 13, 16
Tap dance and membership, 208
Tap Dance Concerto, 52
Tap Dance Instrument, *183*, 191, *192*
Tap Mat, xxi
Tap rhythm, 9, 15, 16
Tap, Rap, 26
Tap, Music for, 205
Tap, rhythm, 65
Tap, Ten Tunes for, 205
Taps, 2
Tenney, James, 159, 181
"Three Little Words," 105-106
Three Monk Tunes, 181
Timbre, 1-2, 55-56
Time signature, 39, 43
   3/4, 66
   5/4, 67
Time Step, 7, 29, 105, 111, 114, 123
   Buggy Ride, 50, 112
   Chug, 119
   Double Five-Sound Wing, 118
   Double Manhattan, 116

one-bar, 9
syncopated, 66
Triple-Triple Cramp Roll, 115
Traveling, 116
Time Step Break, 29-30, 111
   Double Buggy Ride, 113
   Double Fake Wing, 117
   Double Triple Buggy Ride, 113
   Extended, 157
   Half, 115
   Half Fake Wing, 117
   Single Buggy Ride, 112
   Single Syncopated Fake Wing, 118
   traditional, 9
   Traditional Half Triple, 115
   Traditional Single, 114
   Traditional Triple-Triple, 114
   Traveling, 117
   Triple Buggy Ride, 113
   Triple-Triple Buggy Ride, 114
Time Step in Duple Time, Extended, 121
Time Step in a Measure of Five, Bumbishay, 122
Time Steps, Anita's, 119
Tip, xvii, 119
Toe-drop, xvii, 82
   DIG, 67
"Tommy Gun," 84
"Trading Eights," 17, 31
   a capella, 32
   Extended, 32
   Ostinato, 32
   two-bar, 31
Trading Eights dance, 33

Traveling combination, 70
Trenches: see Pulling the
   Trenches.
Triple Paddle and Roll, xvii
Triplet division, 22, 41, 47, 69,
   99, 100
Triplets, 40; half-time, 70
Tufano, Kathryn, *169*
"Twelve Bar Style," 43
"Twister," 182, *183*

"Unsquare Dance," 183, 186

Vierk, Lois V, 181, 182, *192*
Vocabulary, xii

Waller, Fats, 13, 51, 206
Waltz Clog, traditional, 66
Waltz Clog Combination with
   Pullback, Turning, 150
Waltzes, 43
Wayburn, Ned, 155
Weber, Sam, *197*
Whitman Sisters troupe, 105
Wiggins, Jack, 127

Wing, xviii, 127, 137
   Changeover Fake, 143
   Fake, xiv, 143
   Nonchanging Fake, 143
   One-legged 3-sound, 139
   Pendulum, 141
   Toe-Tip Fake, 143
   Turn with 5-sound, 151
   5-tap, 144
   3-sound, xix
   5-sound, xix, 138
   5-tap, 127
   2-legged 3-sound, 138
Wing Break, 5-sound, 119
Wings, Scissor, 142
Wing Combination
   Pendulum, 146
   Scissor, 145
   Three-Sound, 144
Wing Combination with an Over
   the Top, Fake, 147
Woodpeckers Tap Dance Center,
   204

Yancey, Jimmy, 199